Raising Butterflies and Moths in the Garden

Second Edition

BRENDA DZIEDZIC

"There is no better way to develop an emotional connection with the little things that run the world than to nurture butterflies and moths from egg to adult as if they were your own children. With necessary details and lavish illustrations, Brenda Dziedzic shows us how!"

—Dr. Doug Tallamy, Professor of Entomology at the University of Delaware and author of *Bring Nature Home: How Native Plants Sustain Wildlife in Our Gardens*

FIREFLY BOOKS

A FIREFLY BOOK

Published by Firefly Books Ltd. 2023
Copyright © 2023 Firefly Books Ltd.
Text copyright © 2019, 2023 Brenda Sattler
Photographs © as listed on page 391

Maps on pages 24, 42, 52, 66, 80, 102, 116, 122, 130, 136, 146, 150, 158, 182, 192, 198, 206, 218, 228, 236, 254, 268, 276 and 284 from KAUFMAN FIELD GUIDE TO BUTTERFLIES OF NORTH AMERICA. Copyright © 2003 by Hillstar Editions L.C. Reprinted by permission of Houghton Mifflin Harcourt Publishing Company. All rights reserved.

First printing

Library of Congress Control Number: 2022946893

Library and Archives Canada Cataloguing in Publication
Title: Raising butterflies and moths in the garden / Brenda Dziedzic.
Other titles: Raising butterflies in the garden
Names: Dziedzic, Brenda, 1952- author.
Description: Second edition. | Previous edition published under title:
  Raising butterflies in the garden. | Includes bibliographical references and index.
Identifiers: Canadiana 20220435197 | ISBN 9780228104209 (softcover)
Subjects: LCSH: Butterfly gardening—Handbooks, manuals, etc. |
  LCSH: Butterflies—Identification. | LCSH: Moths—Identification. |
  LCGFT: Handbooks and manuals. | LCGFT: Field guides.
Classification: LCC QL544.6 .D95 2023 | DDC 638/.5789—dc23

Published in the United States by
Firefly Books (U.S.) Inc.
P.O. Box 1338, Ellicott Station
Buffalo, New York
14205

Published in Canada by
Firefly Books Ltd.
50 Staples Avenue, Unit 1
Richmond Hill, Ontario
L4B 0A7

Cover and interior design: Stacey Cho

Printed in China

I dedicate this book to
Lois Hansen
who got me started
in this wonderful world
of butterflies.

Contents

Swallowtails

Whites and Sulphurs

Blues

Brushfoots

Skippers

Silk Moths

Sphinx Moths

Tiger Moths

Tussock Moths

Preface

I've always had a love for nature, and in the late summer of 2001, the thought came to me that it would be nice to see more butterflies in my yard, like I used to see when I was a child. What could I do? I decided to create a butterfly garden and went out and bought my first three butterfly bushes. That winter I did a lot of research on the Internet to find out what other kinds of plants I would need. In the early spring of 2002, I took my list of plants to a gardening store to buy seeds. There I met Lois Hansen, and she started me in the right direction to learning about butterflies and moths. She told me that most of the plants on my list would not attract butterflies. She then gave me a list of necessary plants for my garden. I had no idea where to purchase these plants, so Lois gave me several names of native plant nurseries and also offered me some of her plants. A few months later, she brought over plants from her garden and my very first Monarch eggs. She also brought over several books about butterflies for me to read. That was it. I was hooked. From then on I began reading every book I could find about butterflies and moths.

Lois Hansen

Since 2002 I have raised thousands of butterflies and moths. I bring most of the eggs that I find into my house so that I can help the butterflies, because a lot of their habitat is being destroyed. When they come out of their chrysalises, cocoons and pupae, I release them back into the garden. I have gained a lot of knowledge about butterflies and moths by observing their life cycles.

Anyone can have a variety of butterflies and moths in their yard by planting the plants that butterflies and moths use. Even though I have a small city lot, which is 60 feet by 120 feet, I have many different species of butterflies and moths in my yard because of the diversity of host plants I grow. Each year, I increase my variety of host and nectar plants. If the butterflies and moths can complete their life cycles in your yard, you'll have more fluttering about than you would by growing only nectar plants.

I try to share my knowledge about butterfly and moth host plants and raising butterflies and moths with as many people as I can. We need to give back to the earth, and we can do this by planting the native plants that were intended to grow in our areas. Native plants have higher nectar content than most nonnatives, and they produce a healthy ecosystem by attracting a wider variety of birds and insects, which enhances an area's overall biodiversity.

Use caution when handling caterpillars you are unfamiliar with. Some caterpillars have irritating hairs, and some may also use irritating hairs in making their cocoons.

Introduction

Butterflies and moths make up the insect order Lepidoptera. Lepidoptera is derived from the Greek words "lepido" for scale and "ptera" for wings.

The Differences Between Butterflies and Moths

The following are the major differences between butterflies and moths, but there are exceptions too. Butterflies are generally diurnal (day flying), have thin and smooth bodies, hold their wings upright over their backs when at rest, are colorful, and have clubbed antennae. Moths are generally nocturnal (night flying), have fat hair-like scales on their bodies, fold their wings over their backs like tents or wrap them over their bodies when at rest, are dull colored, and have thread-like or feathery antennae.

Butterfly/Moth Life Cycle

Butterflies and moths undergo a complete metamorphosis. This consists of four distinct stages: egg (ovum), caterpillar (larva), chrysalis/pupa and adult (imago).

Egg

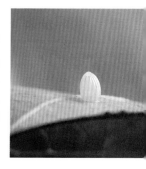

Eggs come in various shapes, colors and sizes. Some of the shapes and textures include barrel, conical, elongated, oval with a flat bottom, spherical, sculptured and smooth. They come in many colors, including beige, cream, green, light green, light yellow, turquoise and white. The egg sizes range from about $\frac{1}{64}$ inch to a little over $\frac{1}{16}$ inch.

Caterpillar

A caterpillar has three parts: the head, thorax and abdomen. The head usually has six pairs of simple eyes (ocelli). Even though caterpillars have so many eyes, their vision is poor. The head also has a spinneret that produces silk. The body consists of 13 segments: three thoracic segments and 10 abdominal segments. The thorax has three pairs of true legs, and the abdomen has five pairs of prolegs (most Geometer moths have two pairs of prolegs). The prolegs have very small hooks that enable the caterpillar to hold onto a leaf or a silk mat. Spiracles are holes in the sides of the thorax and abdomen through which the caterpillar receives oxygen.

The caterpillar goes through between 3 and 10 (typically 5) instars, which are periods of growth between molting (the act of shedding its exoskeleton). It has an exoskeleton, and when it becomes too large for its skin, it molts. Before molting, the caterpillar attaches itself to an object with silk. This helps it to crawl out of its old exoskeleton. After the caterpillar attaches to an object, it stops eating and does not move for about a day. Then it molts. When the caterpillar molts for the last time, the chrysalis or pupa is revealed.

Prechrysalis/Prepupal

Before molting for the last time, the caterpillar empties its gut and seeks out a safe place to make its chrysalis/pupa. A butterfly caterpillar spins a silk pad to which it attaches its rear-most pair of prolegs. Some will hang downward in a J shape, and others will also spin a U-shaped girdle, which they position between their first and second abdominal segments. This holds them upright.

A moth caterpillar, however, does not make a silk pad. Many moth caterpillars spin silk cocoons or bind together pieces of leaves and debris with silk to pupate in. Others will burrow into the soil and make a chamber to pupate in.

Chrysalis/Pupa

During the final molting, the exoskeleton splits and the chrysalis/pupa is revealed. The caterpillar's tissues break down and rearrange within the chrysalis/pupa, and the adult is formed.

Adult

When the butterfly or moth emerges from its chrysalis/pupa, its wings are very small and its body is large. As it pumps blood into its wings, the wings elongate and the body becomes smaller. After a few hours, the wings harden and become dry. The butterfly or moth is then ready for flight.

Butterflies and moths have a hard exoskeleton and three main body parts: the head, thorax and abdomen. The head has two large compound eyes and two antennae. Most have a proboscis, a flexible straw-like structure that is used for drinking nectar and fluids. Butterflies and moths use their antennae for smell, touch and balance. They also smell with sense receptors that are located in their legs and other parts of their bodies.

The thorax has two pairs of scaled wings and three pairs of jointed legs. The abdomen contains the reproductive, digestive and excretory systems. Spiracles are the breathing holes that run along the side of the abdomen. The genitalia are located at the end of the abdomen. The two structures of the male's genitalia are called claspers. The female has a notch. These are easily visible with Monarch butterflies; however, with many species, the structures can be very difficult to see.

Both males and females release pheromones to attract a mate. Some butterflies and moths can mate several times in their lives. The male deposits a package of sperm in the female. As each egg is laid, it passes through the sperm and is fertilized. A female can lay anywhere between several up to hundreds of eggs at a time. For example, a Monarch lays an average of 300 to 500 eggs. In nature, only about 2 percent make it to adulthood.

Male

Female

Mating

Time Period of Each Stage

The life cycles of butterflies and moths are dependent on temperatures and daylight hours. In this book, the period of time mentioned for each stage is an average taken for the particular species. In a cold environment and/or in an area with fewer daylight hours, each stage may take considerably longer.

Range Maps

This book features range maps for each profiled species. On the maps, green indicates the current region of each butterfly and moth.

Parts of the Butterfly and Moth

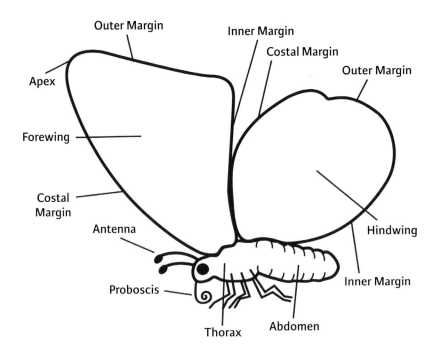

Areas of the Wings

B - basal
PB - postbasal
SMd - submedian
Md - median
PM - postmedian
SMr - submarginal
Mr - marginal
SA - subapical
A - apical

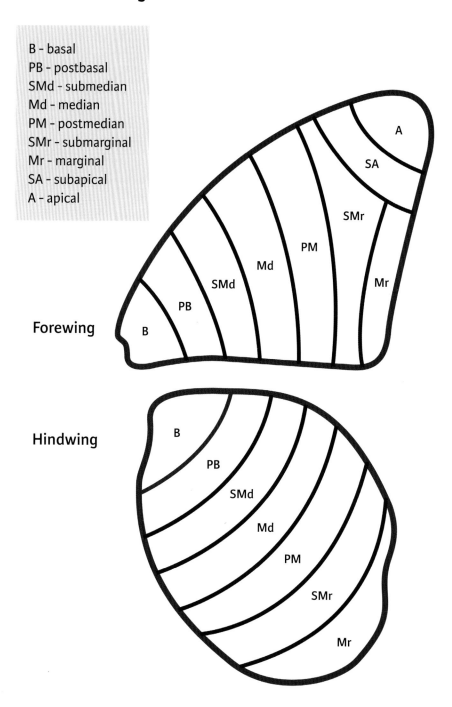

Forewing

Hindwing

Butterfly and Moth Families

Swallowtails

Swallowtails are medium-to-large butterflies, and most have hindwing "tails." As they feed, most flutter their wings. All species visit flowers, and males can be found puddling (drinking liquid nutrients on moist substances). Most males patrol when looking for females. Some perch on high spots instead.

The eggs are usually spherical and smooth.

Many of the young caterpillars mimic bird droppings, with their brownish or blackish-brown bodies and white  dorsal saddles. The caterpillars have an osmeterium, an orangish forked gland behind the head that emits a foul scent to repel predators.

Most of the time, the chrysalises are held upright with a silk girdle. The last brood of the year usually overwinters in the chrysalis stage.

Whites and Sulphurs

Whites and sulphurs are small-to-medium butterflies. All adult species nectar on flowers, and the males often puddle. Males patrol when looking for females.

The eggs are generally elongated.

The caterpillars are usually greenish and covered with very short, fine hair-like scales.

A silken girdle holds the chrysalis upright.

Blues

Blues are very small butterflies. While perched, they rub their hindwings together.

The caterpillars are usually slug-like and produce a sweet liquid called honeydew, which ants eat. The ants, in turn, protect the caterpillars from predators and parasitoids.

Brushfoots

Brushfoots are small-to-large butterflies. This family has more species than any other. All the butterflies in this family have reduced forelegs that are covered with short hair-like scales. The legs look like bottle brushes, hence the name brushfoots.

Males are quite often territorial and aggressive.

Most of the time, brushfoot chrysalises hang downward from a silk pad.

Skippers

Skippers are small-to-medium butterflies. The ends of the clubbed antennae are usually hooked. They have large eyes and stout bodies.

Males look for females by either perching or patrolling.

Adults have an erratic and quick flight.

Silk Moths

Silk moths are small-to-very-large moths. Their bodies are densely covered with hair-like scales. They do not feed because they have reduced or absent proboscises. Many rest with their wings folded vertically over their bodies, while others spread both pairs of wings horizontally.

Some pupate in silken cocoons, and others pupate in soil.

Sphinx Moths

Sphinx moths are small-to-very-large moths. Their wings are usually elongated and narrow. Most have large eyes, which aid them in feeding. Some have very long proboscises, and these help with pollination. Most sphinx moths are very strong fliers and can hover at flowers.

The eggs are usually round, smooth and a shade of green.

The moths usually pupate in soil, but some species will form cocoons in leaf litter.

Tiger Moths

Tiger moths are small-to-medium moths. Many are brightly colored and have spots or geometric shapes on their wings. Their antennae are thread-like. When they rest, their wings are held over the body.

Most tiger moths overwinter as a partially grown caterpillar or as a pupa.

Tussock Moths

Tussock moths are medium moths, with the female usually being larger than the male. Their proboscises are reduced or absent. They often use their larval hairs in the construction of their cocoons.

Butterfly and Moth Gardening Essentials

To attract butterflies and moths to your yard, it is important to plant both nectar and host plants. Nectar plants provide food for the adults that pass through your garden. Make sure you have plants that will blossom in each season, thus providing a continuous food supply.

If you really want them to stay around, then you must plant host plants. These are the plants that the butterflies and moths lay their eggs on and that the caterpillars eat.

Whenever possible, use plants native to your area. Native plants cost less once established because they usually don't require watering, fertilizer or pesticides. They also attract beneficial insects, which reduce pests and pollinate the plants. Additionally, some nonnative plants have been genetically altered so that they have little-to-no nectar. For each butterfly and moth listed in this book, I have also included the Latin names of the host plants, which will help you to select the plants that are native to your area.

Here are some other things to consider in your butterfly garden:

- **Lots of sun.** Most butterfly plants need at least 6 hours of sun each day.
- **Plant arrangements.** To observe the butterflies and moths in your garden easily, plant taller plants behind shorter plants.
- **Plant in groups.** It is easier for butterflies and moths to see plants when they are planted in groups of three or more, because they are nearsighted. When planting host plants, planting in groups will ensure that there is enough food for the caterpillars.
- **Multiple locations for host plants.** To prevent predation of eggs and caterpillars as much as possible, plant host plants in multiple locations.
- **Overripe fruit.** Setting out a container of overripe fruit, such as bananas, cantaloupe, peaches, pears and watermelons, provides nutrients for butterflies and moths. Be sure to expose the juicy insides of the fruit.
- **No pesticides.** The most important thing to remember is that butterflies, moths and caterpillars are insects, so DO NOT USE PESTICIDES.
- **Be wary of Butterfly Bush.** Butterfly Bush is considered invasive in many areas. Some sterile varieties have been developed in order to counteract this issue.

Winter Preparation for Butterfly and Moth Gardens

I live in Westland, Michigan, and I do little to get my garden ready for winter. Various species of butterflies and moths overwinter differently. Some overwinter as eggs, some as larvae, some in chrysalises, naked pupae or pupae within cocoons and some as adults. These wonderful little forms of Lepidoptera could be anywhere in the garden during the winter. They could be on plants, in leaf litter or in the ground. I wait to break down my plants, which I drop to the ground to use as mulch, until sometime in April.

I have many trees, which I grow in pots. I use pots that are 19 inches wide by 16 inches tall. Because of the size of my yard, which is only 60 by 120 feet, I don't have room to plant all of my trees in the ground, but I want to have as many host plants as possible in order to attract a large variety of butterflies and moths.

Over 30 different species of butterflies and moths visit my yard. Some of the trees that I have in pots and the butterflies and moths that lay their eggs on them are:

• Choke Cherry (*Prunus virginiana*) attracts Coral Hairstreak (*Satyrium titus*), Eastern Tiger Swallowtail (*Papilio glaucus*), Giant Leopard Moth (*Hypercompe scribonia*), Io Moth (*Automeris io*), Promethea Moth (*Callosamia promethea*), Red-Spotted Purple (*Limenitis arthemis*) and Striped Hairstreak (*Satyrium liparops*).

- Spicebush (*Lindera benzoin*) attracts Io Moth (*Automeris io*), Promethea Moth (*Callosamia promethea*) and Spicebush Swallowtail (*Papilio troilus*).
- Staghorn Sumac (*Rhus typhina*) attracts Hickory Horned Devil (*Citheronia regalis*) and Luna Moth (*Actias luna*).
- Nannyberry (*Viburnum lentago*) attracts Spring Azure (*Celastrina ladon*), Baltimore Checkerspot (*Euphydryas phaeton*) and Hummingbird Clearwing (*Hemaris thysbe*).
- Sugar Maple (*Acer saccharum*) attracts Cecropia Moth (*Hyalophora cecropia*), Polyphemus Moth (*Antheraea polyphemus*) and Rosy Maple Moth (*Dryocampa rubicunda*).
- Hackberry (*Celtis occidentalis*) attracts American Snout (*Libytheana carinenta*), Hackberry Emperor (*Asterocampa celtis*), Mourning Cloak (*Nymphalis antiopa*), Question Mark (*Polygonia interrogationis*) and Tawny Emperor (*Asterocampa clyton*).
- Black Willow (*Salix nigra*) attracts Dreamy Duskywing (*Erynnis icelus*), Mourning Cloak (*Nymphalis antiopa*), Polyphemus Moth (*Antheraea polyphemus*), Red-Spotted Purple (*Limenitis arthemis*) and Viceroy (*Limenitis archippus*).

To prepare my potted trees for winter, I move them next to my house. I place them right next to each other and put leaves and/or mulch in between, around and over the pots. Putting the plants next to the house and covering them with leaves and mulch helps to protect them from the wind and also keeps the roots warmer. The next spring, when the leaves start growing, I move the trees back to the garden. Whenever my trees start looking distressed, I remove them from their pots and cut the tree down to several inches to reduce the shock of transplanting. Then I cut off about a third of the roots, loosen the roots and repot the trees.

I do have several trees planted in my garden. Each fall I cut them down to 2 to 3 feet tall before there's a chance of frost. By doing this they bush out and stay "Brenda size" (I call them "Brenda size" since I'm only 5-foot-1). The trees that I have planted in the garden are Tulip Poplar, Wild Black Cherry, Hackberry, Hop Tree, Bur Oak, Yellow Birch and Chinquapin Oak.

Raising Butterflies and Moths

If you see a butterfly or moth touching a host plant, that's a good sign that it may be laying eggs. The female will generally curl the anal end of her abdomen as she deposits an egg.

If that is the case, break off a small piece of the leaf that has the egg on it and put it in a container with a lid. When the caterpillar hatches, add leaves as needed. Some other ways to raise caterpillars are by putting a stem of the host plant in a container of water that has a lid with holes just big enough for the stem to go through. You can also put some floral foam (for cut flowers) in a small cup, fill the cup with water, add some stems from the host plant to the floral foam and place it in the habitat, or use a floral tube. Always make sure that the leaves touch the side of the habitat so if the caterpillar falls off the plant, it can easily climb up the sides to get back onto the plant.

It's very important not to let the caterpillars run out of food and also to keep the container clean to prevent health problems.

When a butterfly caterpillar is ready to pupate, it will spin a silk pad to attach its anal prolegs to. Many species will hang downward in a J shape from the silk pad. Swallowtails will also spin a silk girdle, which holds them in an upright position. A moth caterpillar will either start weaving silk to make a cocoon, bury itself under leaves or burrow into the soil. The chrysalises of many butterfly species will become transparent the night before the butterfly emerges, and you'll be able to see the wings. After your butterfly or moth emerges, it will take a few hours for the wings to harden and dry. You can then release it back to your garden. If it is dark or raining, just wait until the next day. They'll be fine without food until then. If it continues to rain for a couple of days, you can feed them Gatorade on a scrunched-up paper towel. (Note that silk moths do not feed because their proboscises are reduced or absent, so there is no need to give them this.) Make sure that you change the paper towel every other day so that bacteria doesn't build up on it. Before reusing your container for another egg or caterpillar, make sure you soak it for at least 15 to 20 minutes in a 10 percent bleach solution, and then rinse the container thoroughly. If possible, dry it in the sun to further sanitize it. This will kill any bacteria or parasites that may be in the container.

That's about all there is to it. Have fun and happy butterflying and mothing!

Black Swallowtail

Papilio polyxenes (pa-pil-ee-oh • pol-ix-ee-nees)

Family

Papilionidae (Swallowtails)
(pap-ill-ee-ON-ah-dee)

Flight period

April–October

Wingspan

2 ½–4 ¼ inches

Identification

Dorsal/Upperside

The dorsal/upperside is black and has an orange hindwing eyespot with a black dot in the middle and a yellow spot near the tip of the forewing. The butterfly has a black body with yellow spots. The male has two rows of yellow spots and a small amount of iridescent blue between the two rows on the hindwing. The female's two rows may be yellow or cream. The submarginal row is reduced and the iridescent blue on the hindwing is increased.

Ventral/Underside

The ventral/underside is black. The forewing has cream spots. The hindwing has cream spots on the marginal edge and two rows of orange spots with iridescent blue between them.

Host/Larval Food Plants

Carrot — *Daucus carota* var. *sativa*
Celery — *Apium graveolens* spp.
Common Rue — *Ruta graveolens*
Dill — *Anethum graveolens*
Fennel — *Foeniculum vulgare* spp.
Golden Alexanders — *Zizia aurea*
Mock Bishop Weed — *Ptilimnium capillaceum*
Parsley — *Petroselinum crispum* spp.
Queen Anne's Lace — *Daucus carota*
Water Cowbane — *Oxypolis filiformis*
Wild Parsnip — *Pastinaca sativa*

Common Rue — *Ruta graveolens*

The Life Cycle

Black Swallowtails have 2 broods each year. The egg is pale yellow and laid singly.

The egg is between ¹⁄₃₂ and ³⁄₆₄ inch. It takes 4 to 8 days for the egg to hatch.

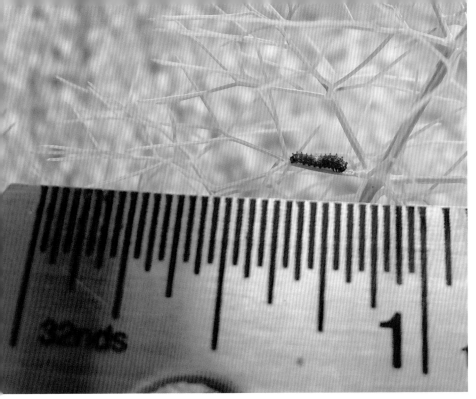

When it hatches, the caterpillar is about ⅛ inch long.

Earlier instars have a cream saddle and branched spines.

After molting, you can see the skin from which it just crawled out and the pale yellow head capsule. Shortly, the head capsule will darken in color. As the caterpillar goes through each instar, its appearance will change.

The caterpillar stage lasts between 14 and 24 days. In the last instar, the caterpillar is about 2 inches long.

When it's ready to pupate, the caterpillar attaches its rear end to a silk pad. It then spins silk threads to form a silk girdle, which holds it upright, in the prechrysalis stage.

When the caterpillar molts for the last time, it reveals its chrysalis.

The chrysalises can be shades of either green or brown, even though the caterpillars eat the same food and make their chrysalises on the same substrate.

The chrysalis stage can be as short as 10 days. If it is the last brood, which overwinters, it will not emerge until spring. There may also be times that the butterfly will not emerge until the following spring.

The chrysalis will become transparent before the adult emerges.

Adult Food

Black Swallowtails can be found puddling, and they also feed on Aster, Azalea, Blazing Star, Blue Mistflower, Brazilian Verbena, Butterfly Bush, Chives, Clover, Garden Phlox, Hyssop, Indian Blanket, Lantana, Milkweed, Monarda, Pentas, Porterweed, Purple Coneflower, Spirea, Sweet William, Thistle and Zinnia.

Blue Mistflower — *Conoclinium coelestinum*

New England Aster — *Symphyotrichum novae-angliae*

Eastern Tiger Swallowtail

Papilio glaucus (pa-pil-ee-oh • glaw-kus)

Family

Papilionidae (Swallowtails)
(pap-ill-ee-ON-ah-dee)

Flight period

April–October

Deep South
February–November

Wingspan

3 ¼–5 ½ inches

Identification

Dorsal/Upperside

The dorsal/upperside of all males and some females is yellow with black tiger stripes. The hindwing has iridescent blue scaling, which is increased on the female. There is also a black form of the female, which is more common southward. The black form has a shadow of tiger stripes.

Ventral/Underside

The ventral/underside of the forewing is similar to the dorsal. It has a row of marginal pale yellow spots and black wing margins. The hindwing has orange marginal spots and iridescent blue scaling.

Host/Larval Food Plants

Ash — *Fraxinus* spp.
Cherry — *Prunus* spp.
Cottonwood — *Populus* spp.
Hop Tree — *Ptelea trifoliata*
Lilac — *Syringa* spp.
Sweet Bay — *Magnolia virginiana*
Tulip Tree — *Liriodendron tulipifera*
Willow — *Salix* spp.

Common lilac — *Syringa vulgaris*

The Life Cycle

Eastern Tiger Swallowtails have 2 to 3 broods each year. The egg is light green, between $\frac{1}{32}$ and $\frac{3}{64}$ inch in width and laid singly on the host leaf. It takes 5 to 10 days for the egg to hatch.

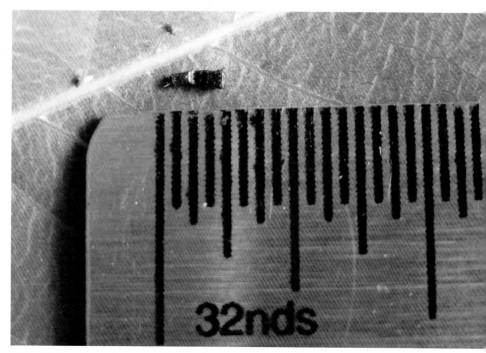

When it hatches, the caterpillar is between $\frac{3}{32}$ and $\frac{1}{8}$ inch long.

The first thing the caterpillar does after hatching is eat its eggshell.

The caterpillar uses the silk it produces to curl a leaf. It stays in that leaf when not eating. Earlier instars resemble bird droppings.

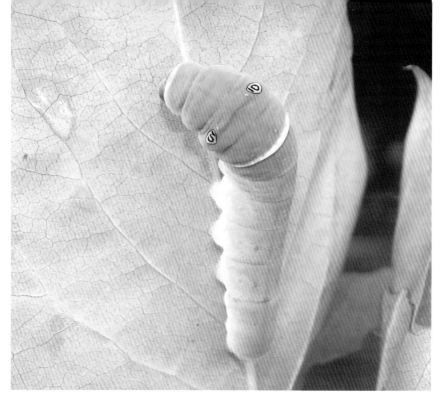

Later instars are snake-like. In the last instar, the caterpillar is about 2 inches long. The caterpillar stage can last up to 46 days.

Right before the prechrysalis stage, the caterpillar turns grayish-brown.

The chrysalis stage can be as short as 10 days. If it is the last brood, which overwinters, it will not emerge until spring. There may also be times that the butterfly will not emerge until the following spring.

Joe-Pye Weed — *Eutrochium purpureum*

Adult Food

Eastern Tiger Swallowtails can be found puddling, and they also feed on Azalea, Blazing Star, Brazilian Verbena, Butterfly Bush, Buttonbush, Chives, Golden Dewdrop, Glossy Abelia, Honeysuckle, Ironweed, Joe-Pye Weed, Lantana, Lilac, Mexican Sunflower, Milkweed, New England Aster, Pentas, Porterweed, Prairie Phlox, Purple Coneflower, Spider Flower, Thistle and Zinnia.

Butterfly Bush — *Buddleia davidii*

Giant Swallowtail

Papilio cresphontes (pa-pil-ee-oh • cres-fon-tees)

Family

Papilionidae (Swallowtails)
(pap-ill-ee-ON-ah-dee)

Flight period

April–October

Deep South
All year

Wingspan

4–6 ¼ inches

Identification

Dorsal/Upperside

The dorsal/upperside is blackish brown. It has a pale yellow band across the forewings and a pale yellow diagonal band that starts at the tip of the forewing and ends at the anal edge of the hindwing. Near the anal edge of the hindwing, there is a reddish-orange spot with blue above it and a black dot below it. The female has more blue above the reddish-orange spot than the male has. The tail of each hindwing has a pale yellow spot.

Ventral/Underside

The ventral/underside is pale yellow with blackish-brown markings and a blue median hindwing band with orange markings on either side.

Host/Larval Food Plants

Citrus — *Citrus* spp.
Common Rue — *Ruta graveolens*
Hercules Club — *Zanthoxylum clava-herculis*
Hop Tree — *Ptelea trifoliata*
Lime Prickly-Ash — *Zanthoxylum fagara*
Common Prickly-Ash — *Zanthoxylum americanum*
Torchwood — *Amyris elemifera*

Common Rue — *Ruta graveolens*

The Life Cycle

Giant Swallowtails have 2 to 3 broods each year. The egg is light yellowish-tan to orangish-brown and laid singly.

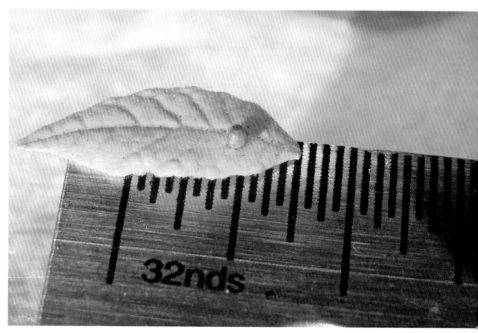

The egg is between $\frac{1}{32}$ and $\frac{3}{64}$ inch wide. It takes 4 to 9 days for the egg to hatch.

When it hatches, the caterpillar is about ⅛ inch long.

After hatching, the caterpillar will eat its eggshell.

The caterpillar looks like bird droppings, which helps deter predators.

The caterpillar stage lasts between 18 and 26 days. In the last instar, the caterpillar is about 2³⁄₁₆ inches long.

The caterpillar attaches its rear end to a silk pad. It then spins silk threads to form a silk girdle, which holds it upright in the prechrysalis stage.

The chrysalis stage can be as short as 14 days. If it is the last brood, which overwinters, it will not emerge until spring. There may also be times that the butterfly will not emerge until the following spring.

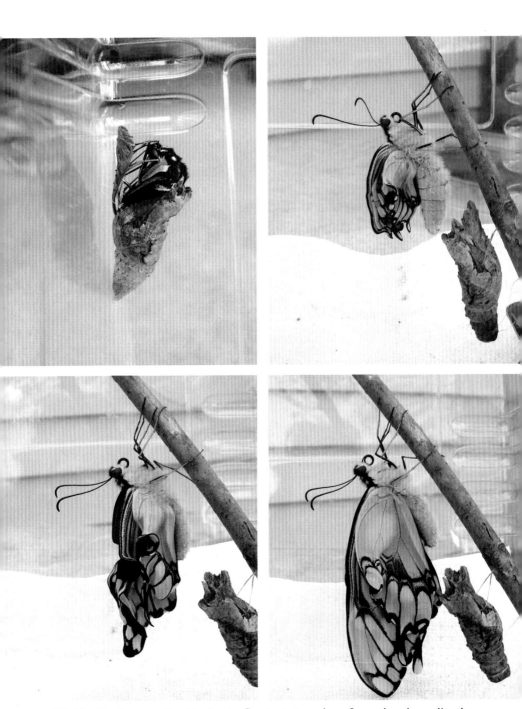

Within 15 minutes after the butterfly starts to eclose from the chrysalis, the wings are completely expanded. It takes a few hours for the wings to harden and dry.

Adult Food

Giant Swallowtails can be found puddling, and they also feed on dung, rotting fruit, Azalea, Brazilian Verbena, Butterfly Bush, Buttonbush, Bougainvilla, Carolina Jasmine, Chives, Citrus, Firespike, Golden Dewdrop, Goldenrod, Joe-Pye Weed, Lantana, Mexican Sunflower, Milkweed, Monarda, Pentas, Porterweed, Purple Coneflower, Scabiosa, Thistle and Zinnia.

Swamp Milkweed — *Asclepias incarnata*

Purple Coneflower — *Echinacea purpurea*

"Profusion Apricot" Zinnia — *Zinnia angustifolia x elegans*

Pipevine Swallowtail

Battus philenor (bat-tus • fil-en-or)

Family

Papilionidae (Swallowtails)
(pap-ill-ee-ON-ah-dee)

Flight period

April–October

Deep South
February–November

Wingspan

2 ¾–4 ½ inches

Identification

Dorsal/Upperside

The dorsal/upperside is black with white marginal spots on the outer margins of both wings. The hindwing of the male is iridescent blue or greenish-blue with submarginal white spots. The female is duller and has more prominent white submarginal spots.

Ventral/Underside

The ventral/underside is black. The forewing is similar to the dorsal. The hindwing has greenish-blue iridescent scales, a row of submarginal orange spots and white marginal spots on the outer margin.

Host/Larval Food Plants

Dutchman's Pipe — *Aristolochia macrophylla*
Swanflower — *Aristolochia erecta*
Virginia Snakeroot — *Aristolochia serpentaria*
Watson's Dutchman's Pipe — *Aristolochia watsonii*
Wooly Pipevine — *Aristolochia tomentosa*

They also use other Pipevine (*Aristolochia* spp.), but proceed with caution when offering *Aristolochia gigantea*. It is toxic to caterpillars in most areas. However, some caterpillars in California have adapted to tolerate this toxicity.

Dutchman's Pipe — *Aristolochia macrophylla*

The Life Cycle

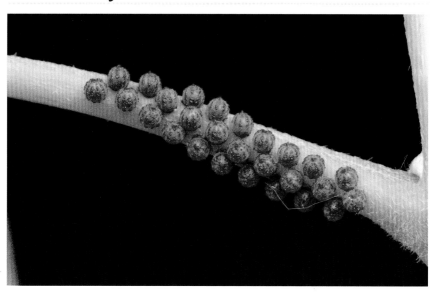

Pipevine Swallowtails have 2 broods each year in the north and 3 to 4 in the deep south. The eggs are brownish-orange and laid singly or in clusters. They lay their eggs on the host plant's tendrils and on both sides of the host leaf.

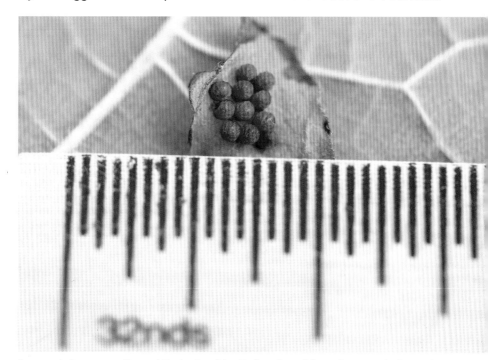

An egg is between 1/32 and 3/64 inch wide. Before hatching, the egg darkens. It takes 4 to 7 days for the egg to hatch.

The caterpillars feed in groups when they're young.

In the last instar, the caterpillar is about 2 ½ inches long. The caterpillar stage lasts between 15 and 30 days.

The caterpillar attaches its rear end to a silk pad. It then spins silk threads to form a silk girdle, which holds it upright in the prechrysalis stage.

The chrysalis color can vary.

The chrysalis stage can be as short as 9 days. If it is the last brood, which overwinters, it will not emerge until spring. There may also be times that the butterfly will not emerge until the following spring.

Adult Food

Pipevine Swallowtails can be found puddling, and they also feed on Alfalfa, Azalea, Brazilian Verbena, Brodiaeas, Butterfly Bush, Buttonbush, California Buckeye, Cleome, Clover, Firebush, Frostweed, Gilias, Globe Amaranth, Golden Corydalis, Ironweed, Joe-Pye Weed, Lantana, Lilac, Lupine, Mexican Sunflower, Milkweed, Monarda, New England Aster, Pentas, Petunia, Phlox, Porterweed, Sand Verbena, Southern Corydalis, Sunflower, Teasel, Thistle, Viper's Bugloss, Yellow Star Thistle, Yerba Santa and Zinnia.

Pentas — *Pentas* **spp.**

Polydamas Swallowtail

Battus polydamas (bat-tus • pah-lee-duh-muss)

Family

Papilionidae (Swallowtails)
(pap-ill-ee-ON-ah-dee)

Flight period

March–December

Wingspan

2 $^{15}/_{16}$–4 $^{1}/_{16}$ inches

Identification

Dorsal/Upperside

The dorsal/upperside is brown with a submarginal pale yellow band.

Ventral/Underside

The ventral/underside is brown. The forewing has a submarginal pale yellow band. The hindwing is brown, has a scalloped margin and a marginal row of red zigzag spots. This swallowtail is tailless.

Host/Larval Food Plants

Pipevine — *Aristolochia* spp.

Pipevine — *Aristolochia* spp.

The Life Cycle

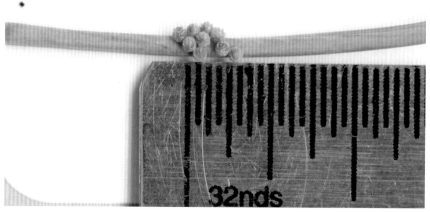

Polydamas Swallowtails have 2 to 3 broods each year. The eggs are orangish and laid in groups on vines, stems and tree bark. They are between 1/32 and 3/64 inch wide.

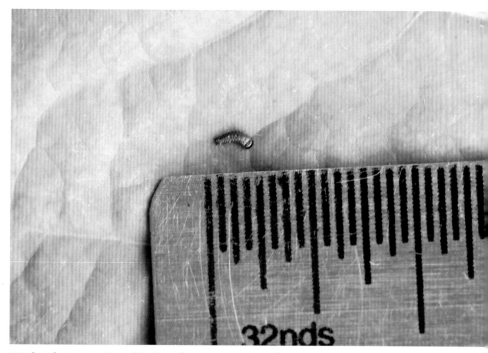

It takes between 5 and 9 days for an egg to hatch.

Young caterpillars feed in groups on the underside of the host leaf.

Caterpillars can vary in color. As they mature, they become solitary.

The caterpillar stage lasts between 18 and 24 days.

The chrysalis stage lasts between 30 and 36 days, except for the last brood, which overwinters and emerges in spring. There may also be times that the butterfly will not emerge until the following spring.

Adult Food

Polydamas Swallowtails nectar on False Heather, Honeysuckle, Lantana, Milkweed, Mistflower, Pentas, Soapweed and Zinnia.

Spicebush Swallowtail

Papilio troilus (pa-pil-ee-oh • troy-lus)

Family

Papilionidae (Swallowtails)
(pap-ill-ee-ON-ah-dee)

Flight period

April–October

Deep South
March–December

Wingspan

3 ½–5 inches

Identification

Dorsal/Upperside

The dorsal/upperside is black with white spots along the marginal edge of the forewing. The hindwing has iridescent bluish scales on the female and iridescent bluish-green scales on the male. There are pale bluish-green spots along the marginal edge.

Ventral/Underside

The ventral/underside is black. The forewing is similar to the dorsal. On the hindwing, there are blue scales along the postmedian band with orange spots on either side. The body has rows of white spots.

Host/Larval Food Plants

Camphor Tree — *Cinnamomum camphora*
Redbay — *Persea borbonia*
Sassafras — *Sassafras albidum*
Spicebush — *Lindera benzoin*

Spicebush — *Lindera benzoin*

The Life Cycle

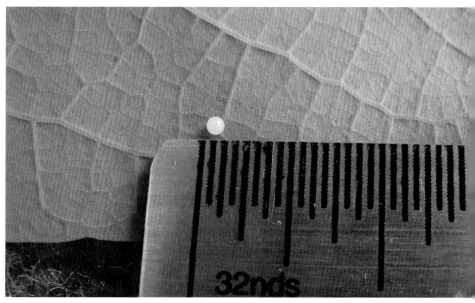

Spicebush Swallowtails have 2 to 3 broods each year. The egg is a pale greenish-white and laid singly on the underside of the host leaf most of the time.

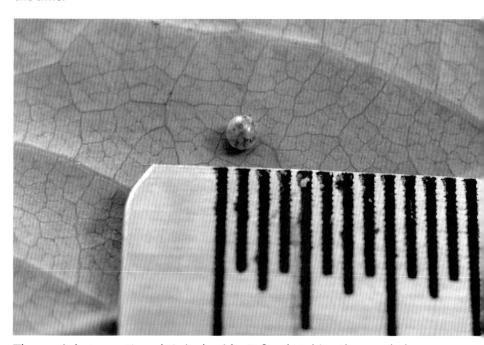

The egg is between $\frac{1}{32}$ and $\frac{3}{64}$ inch wide. Before hatching the egg darkens. It takes between 4 and 8 days for the egg to hatch.

When it hatches, the caterpillar is about 3/32 inch long.

The first thing the caterpillar does after hatching is eat its eggshell. Then the caterpillar will use the silk it produces to curl a leaf, where it stays when it's not eating.

The earlier instars resemble bird droppings.

The later instars are snake-like.

In the last instar, the caterpillar is yellow and is about 2 ³⁄₁₆ inches long. The caterpillar stage lasts between 16 and 20 days.

The chrysalis stage can be as short as 12 days. If it is the last brood, which overwinters, it will not emerge until spring. There may also be times that the butterfly will not emerge until the following spring.

Adult Food

Spicebush Swallowtails can be found puddling, and they also feed on Aster, Azalea, Blazing Star, Brazilian Verbena, Butterfly Bush, Buttonbush, Dogbane, Firebush, French Marigold, Globe Amaranth, Golden Crownbeard, Honeysuckle, Lantana, Lilac, Lupine, Milkweed, Monarda, Pentas, Pineapple Sage, Purple Coneflower, Summer Phlox, Sweet Pepperbush, Thistle and Zinnia.

"Pink Delight" Butterfly Bush — *Buddleia davidii*

Zebra Swallowtail

Eurytides marcellus (eur-ee-tides • mar-sell-us)

Family

Papilionidae (Swallowtails)
(pap-ill-ee-ON-ah-dee)

Flight period

June–August

Deep South
March–December

Wingspan

2½–4 inches

Identification

Dorsal/Upperside

The dorsal/upperside is white with black stripes. The hindwings have very long tails.

Ventral/Underside

The ventral/underside is similar to the dorsal/upperside except there is a red stripe running through the middle of the hindwing.

Host/Larval Food Plants

Pawpaw — *Asimina* spp.

Pawpaw – *Asimina triloba*

The Life Cycle

The Zebra Swallowtail has two broods in the north from April to August and many broods in the south from March to December. The egg is about $\frac{1}{32}$ inch and pale green. It takes about 4 to 6 days for the eggs to hatch.

When the caterpillar hatches, it is about $\frac{3}{32}$ inch.

In the last instar, the caterpillar is about 1 $\frac{15}{16}$ inches long. The body is green with broad blue, black and yellow bands between the thorax and abdomen. The thorax and abdomen usually have yellow, green and black bands. The caterpillar stage can be as long as 22 days.

The chrysalis stage can be as short as 10 days. If it is the last brood, which overwinters, it will not emerge until next spring.

Adult Food

Adults feed on a variety of flowers. They can also be found puddling.

Cabbage White

Pieris rapae (py-er-iss • rap-ee)

Family

Pieridae (White/Sulphur)
(pee-AIR-ri-dee)

Flight period

March–November

South
All year

Wingspan

1¾–2¼ inches

Identification

Dorsal/Upperside

The dorsal/upperside is white. The forewing has a black patch near the apex. The female has two submarginal black spots and the male has one.

Ventral/Underside

The ventral/underside is yellowish-green or grayish-green.

Host/Larval Food Plants

Broccoli — *Brassica oleracea* spp.
Brussel Sprouts — *Brassica oleracea* spp.
Cabbage — *Brassica oleracea* var. *capitata*
Cauliflower — *Brassica oleracea* spp.
Indian Mustard — *Brassica juncea*
Nasturtium — *Tropaeolum* spp.
Peppergrass — *Lepidium virginicum*
Radish — *Raphanus sativus*
Sweet Alyssum — *Lobularia maritima*

Nasturtium — *Tropaeolum* **spp.**

The Life Cycle

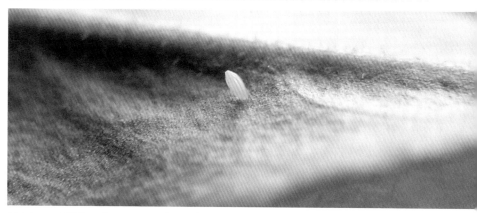

Cabbage Whites have many broods each year. The egg is laid singly.

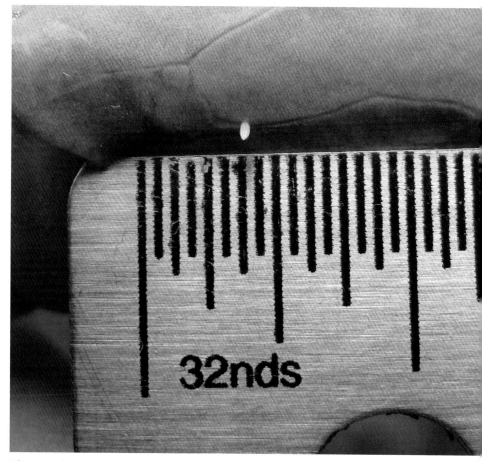

The egg is about 1/64 inch wide and pale yellowish-white. It takes between 3 and 7 days for the egg to hatch.

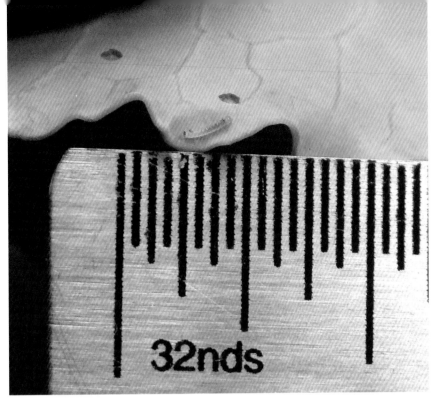

When it hatches, the caterpillar is between 1/16 and 3/32 inch long.

The caterpillar stage lasts for 14 to 20 days. In the last instar, the caterpillar is about 1 3/16 inches long.

The caterpillar attaches its rear end to a silk pad and also secures itself with a silk sling around its thorax before pupating. The chrysalis is jade green at first and then turns yellowish-tan.

The chrysalis stage lasts between 8 and 12 days, except for the last brood, which overwinters and emerges the following spring.

The day before the butterfly emerges, the chrysalis becomes transparent.

Adult Food

Cabbage Whites nectar on Aster, Blazingstar, Blue Mistflower, Brazilian Verbena, Butterfly Bush, Coreopsis, Cosmos, Dandelion, Garden Phlox, Joe-Pye Weed, Mint, Mustard, New England Aster, Purple Coneflower, Red Clover, Salvia, Scabiosa and Scarlet Monkeyflower.

New England Aster — *Symphyotrichum novae-angliae*

Blue Mistflower — *Conoclinium coelestinum*

Great Southern White

Ascia monuste (ash-ee-ah • mo-nus-te)

Family

Pieridae (White/Sulphur)
(pee-AIR-ri-dee)

Flight period

Deep South
All year

Wingspan

1 13/16–3 3/8 inches

Identification

Dorsal/Upperside

The dorsal/upperside of the male is white. It has a black zigzag marking on the outer margin. There are two forms of females. One form is similar to the male, except it has wider zigzag markings and a small black cell spot on the forewing. The other form has dark scales. Both sexes have turquoise antennal clubs.

Ventral/Underside

The ventral/underside of the male is white or pale yellow. One form of the female is similar to the male. The other form has a pale brown or smoky gray underside.

Host/Larval Food Plants

Arugula — *Eruca* spp.
Bayleaf Caper Tree — *Capparis flexuosa*
Cabbage — *Brassica oleracea* var. *capitata*
Caper — *Capparis* spp.
Coastal Searocket — *Cakile lanceolata*
Collard Greens — *Brassica oleracea* var. *acephala*
Garlic Pear Tree — *Crataeva tapia*
Mustard Greens — *Brassica juncea*
Nasturtium — *Tropaeolum* spp.
Peppergrass — *Lepidium virginicum*
Redwhisker Clammyweed — *Polanisia dodecandra*
Saltwort — *Batis maritima*
Spider Flower — *Cleome hassleriana*
Tansy Mustard — *Descurainia pinnata brachycarpa*
Watercress — *Nasturtium officinale*

Spider Flower — *Cleome hassleriana*

The Life Cycle

Great Southern Whites have several broods each year. The eggs are pale yellow and usually laid in groups on the top of the host leaf.

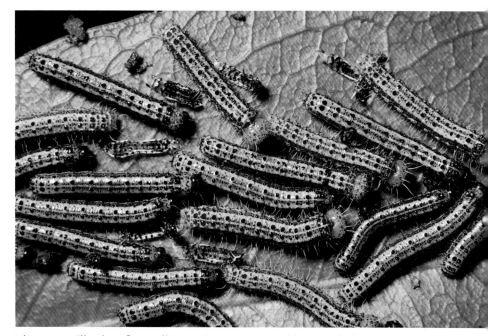

The caterpillar has five yellow stripes, separated by mottled gray, that run the length of its body. All over the body there are small and large black spots.

The caterpillar is on Watercress (*Nasturtium officinale*).

In the last instar, the caterpillar is about 2 inches long.

Adult Food

Great Southern Whites nectar on Butterfly Bush, Coneflower, Daisy, Gumweed, Indian Blanket, Lantana, Milkweed, Mistflower, Saltwort, Salvia, Spanish Needle, Verbena and Zinnia.

Yellow Lantana — *Lantana* **spp.**

Orange Sulphur

Colias eurytheme (co-lee-as • yur-ee-theme)

Family

Pieridae (White/Sulphur)
(pee-AIR-ri-dee)

Flight period

March–December

Wingspan

1 9/16–2 9/16 inches

Identification

Dorsal/Upperside

The dorsal/upperside is yellow. There is a solid black border on the male and an uneven black border with a few yellow spots on the female. Both have a black spot near the top edge of the forewing and a central orange spot on the hindwing. There is also a white form of the female with the same markings as the yellow form.

Ventral/Underside

The ventral/underside is yellow with pink wing edges and a silver spot rimmed with pink on the hindwing.

Host/Larval Food Plants

Alfalfa — *Medicago sativa*
Bush Clover — *Lespedeza* spp.
Red Clover — *Trifolium pratense*
Vetch — *Vicia* spp.
White Clover — *Trifolium repens*
White Sweet Clover — *Melilotus albus*

Red Clover — *Trifolium pratense*

The Life Cycle

Orange Sulphurs have several broods each year. The egg is cream-colored and laid singly on the host leaf. It turns reddish-orange as the caterpillar develops.

The egg is between $\frac{1}{64}$ and $\frac{1}{32}$ inch wide. It takes 4 to 8 days for the egg to hatch.

When the caterpillar hatches, it is about 1/16 inch long.

In the last instar, the caterpillar is about 1⅜ inches long. The caterpillar stage lasts between 14 and 28 days.

Prechrysalis

When the chrysalis is first revealed, it is green. It turns yellow as it hardens. Before the butterfly emerges, the chrysalis becomes transparent. It is in the chrysalis for as few as 7 days. Because the last brood overwinters, some are in the chrysalis until spring.

The Orange Sulphur is emerging from its chrysalis.

Adult Food

Orange Sulphurs can be found puddling, and they also feed on Alfalfa, Aster, Blazing Star, Brazilian Verbena, Butterfly Bush, Clover, Dandelion, Dogbane, Garden Phlox, Goldenrod, Hyssop, Marigold, Mexican Sunflower, Milkweed, Mint, Sedum and Winter Cress.

Marigold — *Tagetes* **spp.**

Butterfly Bush — *Buddleia davidii*

Eastern Tailed-Blue

Cupido comyntas (cue-pih-doh • co-min-tahs)

Family

Lycaenidae (Blues)
(lie-SEEN-ah-dee)

Flight period

February–November

Wingspan

½–1 ⅛ inches

Identification

Dorsal/Upperside

The dorsal/upperside of the male is purplish-blue and the female is brownish-gray. Both sexes have one or two orange spots with a black dot above the tail on the hindwing.

Ventral/Underside

The ventral/underside is pale bluish-gray with several blackish-gray spots and bands. The hindwing has one to three orange spots with a black dot above the tail.

Host/Larval Food Plants

Alfalfa — *Medicago sativa*
Bush Clover — *Lespedeza* spp.
Clover — *Trifolium* spp.
Lupine — *Lupinus* spp.
Sweet Clover — *Melilotus* spp.
Tick-Trefoil — *Desmodium* spp.
Vetch — *Vicia* spp.
Wild Pea — *Lathyrus* spp.

Red Clover — *Trifolium pratense*

The Life Cycle

Eastern Tailed-Blues have many broods each year. The egg is laid singly on flowers and young leaves. The egg is pale green.

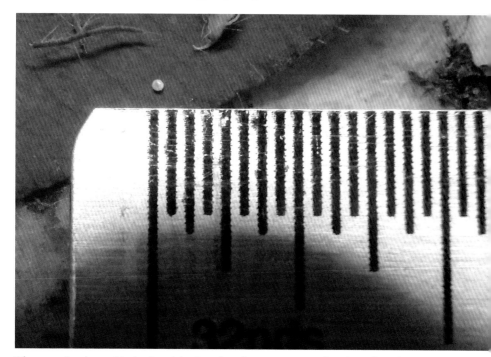

The egg is about 1/64 inch wide. It takes between 3 and 6 days for the egg to hatch.

When the caterpillar hatches, it is about ³⁄₆₄ inch long. It will feed on buds, flowers, seeds and young leaves.

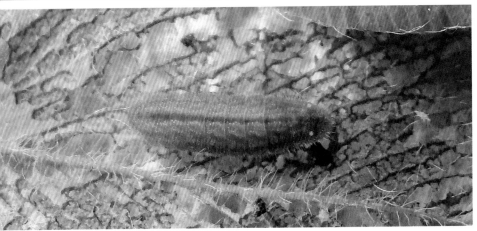

The caterpillars vary in color, anywhere between green and reddish-brown.

The white skin behind this caterpillar reveals that it has just finished molting. In the last instar, the caterpillar is about ⅜ inch long. The caterpillar stage lasts for 18 to 24 days, except for the last brood, which overwinters in the last instar. It may overwinter in seedpods from the host plant it has been feeding on.

Chrysalises vary in color from light green to dark green to reddish-brown.

The chrysalis stage lasts for 3 to 5 days.

The chrysalis becomes transparent before the butterfly emerges.

Adult Food

Male Eastern Tailed-Blues can be found puddling. Some of the plants that both males and females nectar on include Aster, Brazilian Verbena, Butterfly Bush, Cinquefoil, Dogbane, Goldenrod, Joe-Pye Weed, Milkweed, Mint, Red Clover, Shepherd's Needle, White Sweet Clover, Wild Strawberry, Winter Cress and Yarrow.

New England Aster — *Symphyotrichum novae-angliae*

Karner Blue

Lycaeides melissa samuelis (ly-see-ih-dees • me-lis-ah • sam-u-el-is)

Family

Lycaenidae (Blues)
(lie-SEEN-ah-dee)

Flight period

May–August

Wingspan

1 inch

Identification

Dorsal/Upperside

The dorsal/upperside of the male is silvery or violet-blue. It has a narrow black margin with a white outer fringe. The female is grayish-brown with purplish-blue near the body and has a row of orange crescents near the edge of the hindwing.

Ventral/Underside

The ventral/underside of both the male and female is gray with a row of orange crescents along the wing margin and black spots circled with white.

Host/Larval Food Plants

Wild Lupine — *Lupinus perennis*

Wild Lupine — *Lupinus perennis*

The Life Cycle

Karner Blues have 2 broods each year. The egg is laid singly on leaves, stems and in leaflitter close to the Lupine. The egg is pale green and slightly larger than $\frac{1}{32}$ inch. It takes between 5 and 10 days for the egg to hatch. The eggs of the 2nd brood overwinter.

The caterpillar is slug-like. When young, it is a pale yellowish-green.

The caterpillar eats the leaf's mesophyll and leaves the epidermis, which creates a pattern on the leaf. This is called "window paning." In the last instar, the caterpillar is about $^{15}/_{16}$ inch long. The caterpillar stage lasts for 3 to 4 weeks.

The chrysalis stage lasts for 5 to 12 days. The adult butterfly usually lives between 4 and 7 days, but it can live up to several weeks.

Adult Food

Karner Blues can be found puddling, and they also feed on dung, Aster, Bastard Toadflax, Bedstraw, Bird's Foot Violet, Black-Eyed Susan, Butterfly Weed, Bachelors Button, Balsam Ragwort, Common Evening Primrose, Common Milkweed, Common Yarrow, Cottonweed, Cream Wild Indigo, Cylindrical Blazing Star, False Spikenard, Fameflower, Fern-Leaved False Foxglove, Flowering Spurge, Frostweed, Goat's Rue, Golden Alexander, Grass-Leaved Goldenrod, Harebell, Hoary Puccoon, Horsemint, Lance-Leaved Coreopsis, Lead Plant, Long-Leaved Bluets, Lyre Leaved Sand Cress, New Jersey Tea, Ohio Spiderwort, Old Field Goldenrod, Pale Spiked Lobelia, Prairie Coreopsis, Prairie Phlox, Purple Milkwort, Purple Prairie Clover, Rough Blazing Star, Round Headed Bush Clover, Showy Goldenrod, Starry False Solomens Seal, Swamp Milkweed, Sweet Everlasting, Thimbleweed, Thyme Leaved Sandwort, Toad Flax, Two-Flowered Cynthia, Upland White Aster, Western Sunflower, White Prairie Clover, Whorled Milkweed, Wild Bergamot, Wild Geranium, Wild Lupine, Wild Strawberry, Wood Betony and Woodland Sunflower.

Wild Geranium — *Geranium maculatum*

Summer Azure

Celastrina neglecta (sel-ah-stree-nah • ne-glek-tah)

Family

Lycaenidae (Blues)
(lie-SEEN-ah-dee)

Flight period

May–October

Wingspan

⅞–1 ¼ inches

Dorsal/Upperside

The dorsal/upperside is pale blue. The male's forewing has a thin, dark margin. Its hindwing has a dusting of white scales. The dark margin on the female's forewing is wider and the hindwing has a greater amount of white scales.

Ventral/Underside

The ventral/underside is chalky white with small, dark marks and spots.

Host/Larval Food Plants

Cherry — *Prunus* spp.
Dogwood — *Cornus* spp.
Hog-Peanut — *Amphicarpaea bracteata*
Meadowsweet — *Spiraea* spp.
New Jersey Tea — *Ceanothus americanus*
Steeplebush — *Spiraea tomentosa*
Sumac — *Rhus* spp.
Wild Hydrangea — *Hydrangea arborescens*
Wingstem — *Verbesina alternifolia*

New Jersey Tea — *Ceanothus americanus*

The Life Cycle

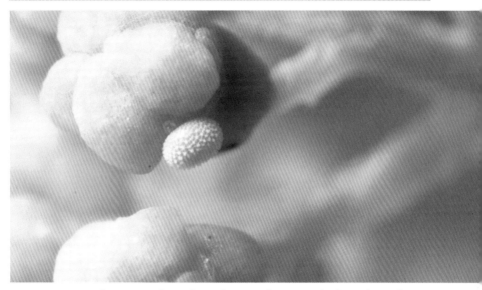

Summer Azures have 1 to 3 broods each year. The egg is laid singly on flower buds and leaf buds. It is greenish-white and about ⅟₃₂ inch wide. It takes between 3 and 5 days for the egg to hatch.

The caterpillar is slug-like and blends into the host plant. It feeds on the flowers and buds. A sugary substance, honeydew, is secreted from its dorsal glands. Ants protect the caterpillar from predators and parasites in return for the honeydew.

The caterpillar stage lasts for 19 to 23 days. In the last instar, the caterpillar is about $^{19}\!/_{32}$ inch long.

The chrysalis stage lasts for 9 to 12 days, except for the last brood which overwinters.

Adult Food

Summer Azures can be found puddling, and they also nectar on Brazilian Verbena, Blue Mistflower, Clover, Daisy, Dogbane, Dogwood, Joe-Pye Weed, Meadowsweet, Milkweed, New Jersey Tea, Pussytoes, Red Bud, Spirea, Steeplebush and Sumac.

Joe-Pye Weed — *Eutrochium purpureum*

American Lady

Vanessa virginiensis (van-ess-ah • ver-jin-ee-in-sis)

Family

Nymphalidae (Brushfoots)
(nim-FAL-ah-dee)

Flight period

April–November

Deep South
All year

Wingspan

1 ¾–2 ⅝ inches

Identification

Dorsal/Upperside

The dorsal/upperside is mainly orange. The forewing has black marks and white spots near the apex. The hindwing has a black band and black marks near the outer margin. Near the submarginal area, there are four black spots. The two outer spots have blue in the middle.

Ventral/Underside

The ventral/underside is brown with a cream cobweb pattern. There are two large eyespots on the hindwing, pink markings on the forewing and a narrow lavender band near the outer margins of both.

Host/Larval Food Plants

Curry Plant — *Helichrysum angustifolium*
Licorice Plant — *Helichrysum petiolare*
Pearly Everlasting — *Anaphalis margaritacea*
Pussytoes — *Antennaria* spp.
Silver Brocade — *Artemisia stelleriana*
Sweet Everlasting — *Pseudognaphalium obtusifolium*

Pearly Everlasting — *Anaphalis margaritacea*

Silver Brocade — *Artemisia stelleriana*

The Life Cycle

American Ladies have 3 to 4 broods each year. The eggs are usually laid singly, but sometimes you will see a couple together.

The egg is about 1/64 inch wide and pale yellowish-green. It takes 3 to 6 days for the egg to hatch.

When the caterpillar hatches, it is between 1/16 and 3/32 inch long.

The caterpillar creates a protective nest by silking together the host plant's leaves, which it eats.

The caterpillar's appearance can vary.

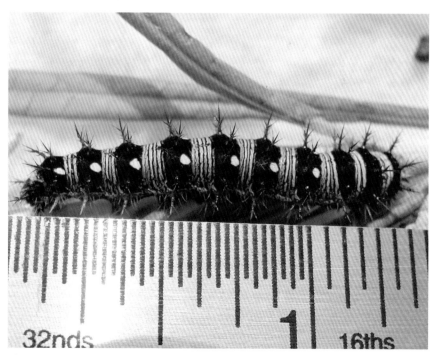

The caterpillar stage lasts for 18 to 22 days. In the last instar, the caterpillar is about 1 ⅝ inches long.

The caterpillar will hang in a J shape for about 24 hours before pupating.

The chrysalis stage lasts for 8 to 12 days. The day before the butterfly emerges, the chrysalis becomes transparent.

Adult Food

American Ladies feed on Aster, Black-Eyed Susan, Brazilian Verbena, Butterfly Bush, Coreopsis, Dogbane, Goldenrod, Heliotrope, Hyssop, Indian Hemp, Marigold, Milkweed, Phlox, Purple Coneflower, Scabiosa, Selfheal, Vetch, Yarrow and Zinnia.

Black-Eyed Susan — *Rudbeckia hirta*

Butterfly Bush — *Buddleia davidii*

Baltimore Checkerspot

Euphydryas phaeton (u-fee-dry-as • fay-ton)

Family

Nymphalidae (Brushfoots)
(nim-FAL-ah-dee)

Flight period

May–August

Wingspan

1 ¾–2 ¾ inches

Identification

Dorsal/Upperside

The dorsal/upperside is black with several rows of cream-white spots toward the outer edge, a row of reddish-orange spots along the outer wing margins and reddish-orange spots toward the base.

Ventral/Underside

The ventral/underside has orange spots along the outer edge, then several rows of cream-white spots. Closer to the basal area, there is a mixture of orange and white spots.

Host/Larval Food Plants

The caterpillars overwinter in the 4th instar. Before overwintering, they use these plants:

English Plantain — *Plantago lanceolata*
Hairy Beardtongue — *Penstemon hirsutus*
Turtlehead — *Chelone glabra*
Yellow False Foxglove — *Aureolaria* spp.

After overwintering, they may also feed on these plants:

Honeysuckle — *Lonicera* spp.
Lousewort — *Pedicularis canadensis*
Viburnum – *Viburnum* spp.
White Ash — *Fraxinus americana*

Turtlehead — *Chelone glabra*

The Life Cycle

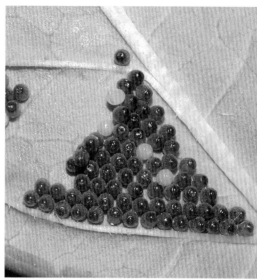

Baltimore Checkerspots have 1 brood each year. The eggs are about 1/32 inch wide and laid in a mass. When first laid, the eggs are yellow. In a couple days they turn light orange, and then reddish. It takes about 2 to 3 weeks for the eggs to hatch.

After the caterpillars hatch, they build a silken bag-like nest in which they eat communally. They overwinter in the 4th instar.

In the spring, the caterpillars wander off and feed solitarily. The caterpillar stage lasts for 10 to 14 days. In the last instar, the caterpillar is about 1 ¾ inches long.

The chrysalis stage lasts for 9 to 12 days.

Adult Food

Baltimore Checkerspots nectar on Dogbane, Indian Blanket, Lobelia, Milkweed, Purple Coneflower, Swamp Thistle, Viburnum and Wild Rose.

Milkweed — *Asclepias* **spp.**

Common Buckeye
Junonia coenia (joo-no-nee-ah • see-nee-ah)

Family

Nymphalidae (Brushfoots)
(nim-FAL-ah-dee)

Flight period

May–October

Deep South
All year

Wingspan

1½–2¾ inches

Identification

Dorsal/Upperside

The dorsal/upperside is brown. The forewing has two eyespots, a white patch and two small orange bars. The hindwing has two eyespots, a light brownish border and an orange margin just inside of the border.

Ventral/Underside

The ventral/underside of the forewing and hindwing is similar to the dorsal, except it is duller.

Host/Larval Food Plants

American Blueheart — *Buchnera americana*
Butter and Eggs — *Linaria vulgaris*
False Foxglove — *Agalinis* spp.
Firecracker — *Russelia* spp.
Frogfruit — *Phyla* spp.
Green Shrimp — *Blechum pyramidatum*
Indian Paintbrush — *Castilleja* spp.
Plantain — *Plantago* spp.
Snapdragon — *Antirrhinum* spp.
Snapdragon Vine — *Maurandya antirrhiniflora*
Sticky Monkeyflower — *Mimulus aurantiacus*
Toadflax — *Linaria* spp.
Twinflower — *Dyschoriste oblongifolia*
Wild Petunia — *Ruellia* spp.
Yaupon Blacksenna — *Seymeria cassioides*

Yaupon Blacksenna — *Seymeria cassioides*

English Plantain — *Plantago lanceolata*

Butter and Eggs — *Linaria vulgaris*

The Life Cycle

Common Buckeyes have several broods each year. The eggs are usually laid singly, but sometimes you will see a couple together.

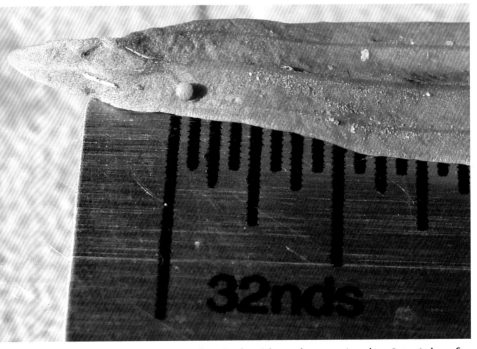

The egg is between $\frac{1}{64}$ and $\frac{1}{32}$ inch wide and green. It takes 3 to 6 days for the egg to hatch.

When the caterpillar hatches, it is about 1/16 inch long.

The caterpillar stage lasts for 12 to 16 days. In the last instar, the caterpillar is about 1¾ inches long.

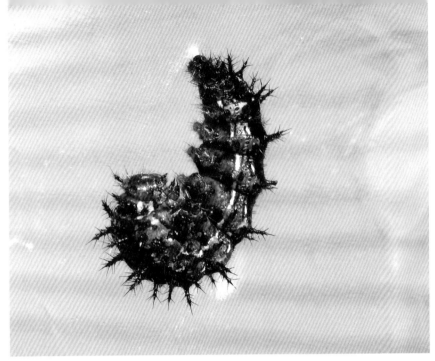

The caterpillar attaches to a silk pad with its cremaster. It then hangs in a J shape for about 24 hours before pupating.

It takes about 1 minute to pupate.

The chrysalis stage lasts for 7 to 10 days, except for the last brood in the south, which overwinters.

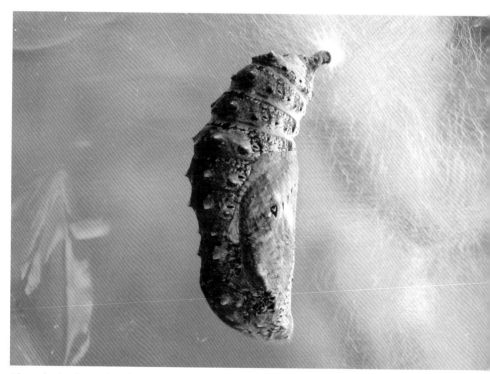

Shortly before the butterfly emerges, the chrysalis becomes slightly transparent.

The adult lives about 10 days, except for those that overwinter in the south.

Red Clover — *Trifolium pratense*

Adult Food

Common Buckeyes often can be seen puddling, and they also feed on carrion, dung, rotten fruit, Aster, Brazilian Bachelor's Button, Brazilian Verbena, Butterfly Bush, California Buckwheat, Chickory, Clover, Cosmos, Dogbane, Frogfruit, Gumweed, Knapweed, Lantana, Milkweed, Peppermint and Tickseed Sunflower.

Brazilian Bachelor's Button — *Centratherum intermedium*

Common Wood-Nymph

Cercyonis pegala (ser-see-oh-nis • peg-ah-la)

Family

Nymphalidae (Brushfoots)
(nim-FAL-ah-dee)

Flight period

May–October

Wingspan

1⅞–3 inches

Identification

Dorsal/Upperside

The dorsal/upperside is dark brown with two black eyespots encircling a small white spot on the forewing. Some have yellow patches around the eyespots.

Ventral/Underside

The ventral/underside is brown. Some have yellow patches around the eyespots and a small white dot within. There are several small eyespots on the hindwing.

Host/Larval Food Plants

Beardgrass — *Bothriochloa* spp.
Bluegrass — *Poa* spp.
Bluestem — *Andropogon* spp.
Purpletop Tridens — *Tridens flavus*
Wild Oat — *Avena fatua*

Big Bluestem — *Andropogon gerardii*

The Life Cycle

Common Wood-Nymphs have 1 brood each year. The eggs are pale yellow or white. They lay their eggs singly on or near the host plant. As it develops, the egg will change to tan, then orangish-brown or have pinkish mottling.

When the caterpillar hatches, it does not eat. Instead, it goes into hibernation. The following year it will complete its life cycle.

In the last instar, the caterpillar is about 2 inches long.

Adult Food

Common Wood-Nymphs can be found puddling, and they also feed on dung, fungi, rotten fruit, tree sap, Alfalfa, Aster, Blue Vervain, Boneset, Brazilian Verbena, Butterfly Bush, Button Bush, Cherry Blossoms, Clover, Fleabane, Goldenrod, Hyssop, Ironweed, Joe-Pye Weed, Lantana, Milkweed, Mint, Monarda, Purple Coneflower, Sunflower and Thistle.

Eastern Comma

Polygonia comma (pol-ih-go-nee-ah • com-ah)

Family

Nymphalidae (Brushfoots)
(nim-FAL-ah-dee)

Flight period

March–October

Wingspan

1 ¾–2 ½ inches

Identification

Dorsal/Upperside

The dorsal/upperside of the forewing is orange with black spots and a black border. The hindwing of the summer form (spring or summer brood) is mostly black, and the hindwing of the winter form (late-summer or fall brood) is mostly orange.

Ventral/Underside

The ventral/underside looks like a dead leaf. The hindwing has a curved silvery spot that resembles a comma.

Host/Larval Food Plants

Elm — *Ulmus* spp.
False Nettle — *Boehmeria cylindrica*
Hackberry — *Celtis* spp.
Hops — *Humulus* spp.
Nettle — *Urtica* spp.
Wood Nettle — *Laportea canadensis*

False Nettle — *Boehmeria cylindrica*

Common Hop — *Humulus lupulus*

The Life Cycle

Eastern Commas have 2 broods each year. The eggs are green and laid singly or stacked.

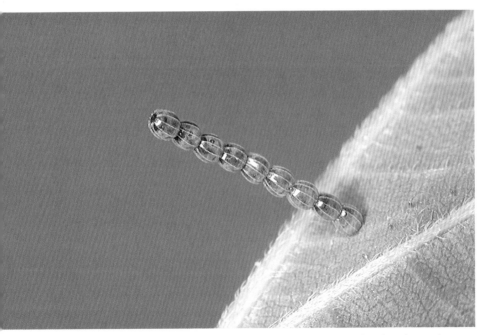

The egg is between 1/64 and 1/32 inch wide. As the caterpillar develops, the egg darkens. It takes between 4 and 6 days for the egg to hatch.

The caterpillars usually eat at night. Older caterpillars make shelters by stitching leaf edges together with silk. Their coloring can vary between the caterpillars shown above and below.

The caterpillar stage lasts for 19 to 22 days. The 2nd brood usually stays longer in the caterpillar stage. In the last instar, the caterpillar is about 1 9/16 inches long.

In preparation for the chrysalis stage, the caterpillar hangs in a J shape.

The chrysalis stage lasts for 7 to 11 days.

Some adults of the winter form will overwinter. They will hibernate in hollow logs, wood piles, crevices in trees, earthen crevices, under bark or under shingles. Others will migrate south for the winter. On warm, sunny days in the winter they may be seen flying around. The adults can live up to 8 months.

Adult Food

Eastern Commas are often seen puddling, and they also feed on dung, rotting fruit, tree sap, Butterfly Bush, Dandelion, Joe-Pye Weed, Milkweed, Purple Coneflower, Showy Stonecrop and Smooth Sumac.

Rotting fruit

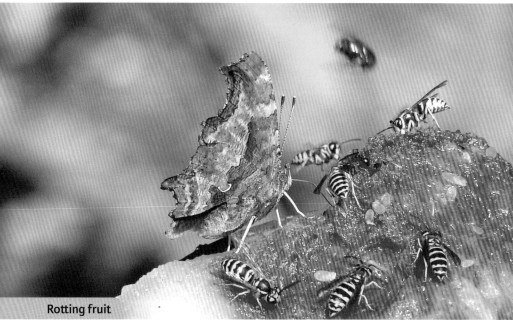

Rotting fruit

Great Spangled Fritillary

Speyeria cybele (spay-er-ee-ah • sib-el-ee)

Family

Nymphalidae (Brushfoots)
(nim-FAL-ah-dee)

Flight period

June–September

Wingspan

2½–4 inches

Identification

Dorsal/Upperside

The dorsal/upperside is orange with heavy black lines and spots.

Ventral/Underside

The ventral/underside of the forewing is similar to the dorsal. The hindwing is orange with silver spots and a yellowish submarginal band.

Host/Larval Food Plants

Violet — *Viola* spp.

Violet — *Viola* spp.

The Life Cycle

Great Spangled Fritillaries have 1 brood each year. The female will walk under the violets as she deposits her eggs. Only a few eggs may actually end up on the plants. Most will be near them.

As the egg develops it darkens. The egg stage lasts for 3 to 4 days.

When the caterpillar hatches from the egg the only thing that it will consume, other than its eggshell, is water. It will then overwinter.

In the spring, when the violets begin to grow, the caterpillar will come out of hibernation. It will then start eating, which it only does at night. In the last instar, the caterpillar is about 2 3/16 inches long.

The chrysalis stage lasts for 9 to 18 days.

Adult Food

Some of the flowers that Great Spangled Fritillaries nectar on include Blazing Star, Butterfly Bush, Coreopsis, Dogbane, Ironweed, Joe-Pye Weed, Lantana, Lavender, Mexican Sunflower, Milkweed, Monarda, Mountain Laurel, Purple Coneflower, Red Clover, Thistle, Verbena, Vetch, White Snakeroot and Zinnia.

Butterfly Bush — *Buddleia davidii*

Gulf Fritillary

Agraulis vanillae (a-grau-liss • va-nil-lee)

Family

Nymphalidae (Brushfoots)
(nim-FAL-ah-dee)

Flight period

March–November

Deep South
All year

Wingspan

2 ½–3 ¾ inches

Identification

Dorsal/Upperside

The dorsal/upperside is bright orange with black markings. There are three small white spots outlined with black on the forewing.

Ventral/Underside

The ventral/underside is brown or brownish-orange with orange at the base of the forewing. There are elongated silvery spots on the hindwing and also on the edge of the forewing.

Host/Larval Food Plants

All Passion-Vine (*Passiflora* spp.), except Red Passion Flower (*Passiflora racemosa* and *Passiflora coccinea*), which is toxic to them and causes death.

Passion-Vine — *Passiflora* spp.

Passion-Vine — *Passiflora* spp.

The Life Cycle

Gulf Fritillaries have several broods each year. The eggs are yellow and laid singly on the leaves or tendrils. As the caterpillar develops, the egg turns reddish-brown. It takes 4 to 8 days for the egg to hatch.

Their appearance can vary. In the last instar, the caterpillar is about 1 ¾ inches long. The caterpillar stage can last as few as 10 days or more than 48 days.

In the prechrysalis stage, the caterpillar hangs in a J shape. The chrysalis stage lasts between 5 and 10 days.

The adult lives up to 6 months and overwinters in the south.

Adult Food

Gulf Fritillaries feed on carrion, dung, Aster, Butterfly Bush, Cordia, Cowpen Daisy, Drummond Phlox, False Heather, Firebush, Goldeneye, Hibiscus, Lantana, Mexican Flame Vine, Pentas, Porterweed, Shepherd's Needle, Spanish Needles, Stokes Aster, Thistle, Tread Softly, Verbena and Zinnia.

Julia Heliconian

Dryas iulia (dry-as • u-lee-ah)

Family

Nymphalidae (Brushfoots)
(nim-FAL-ah-dee)

Flight period

Deep South
All year

Wingspan

3–3 ⅝ inches

Identification

Dorsal/Upperside

The dorsal/upperside of the male is bright orange with black spots toward the apex. The female is dull orange with a black bar across the apex. The hindwing of the male and female has a narrow black margin.

Ventral/Underside

The ventral/underside is light brownish-orange with a pale band through the center.

Host/Larval Food Plants

All Passion-Vine (*Passiflora* spp.), except Red Passion Flower (*Passiflora racemosa* and *Passiflora coccinea*), which is toxic to them and causes death.

Passion-Vine — *Passiflora* spp.

The Life Cycle

The adult female Julia Heliconian prefers to lay her eggs in a shady location.

They have several broods each year. The eggs are yellow and laid on tendrils or leaves, and they are about 1/32 inch. It takes 4 to 6 days for the eggs to hatch, and as they develop they turn a dark orangish color.

In the last instar, the caterpillar is about 1¾ inches.

The chrysalis is a tannish-brown.

Adult Food

Julia Heliconians can be found puddling, and they also feed on pollen, Brazilian Verbena, Butterfly Bush, Coneflower, Firebush, Ghost Plant, Lantana, Large-flower Mexican Clover, Mexican Sunflower, Mistflower, Pentas, Porterweed, Spanish Needles, White Beggar-Ticks and Zinnia.

Firebush — *Hamelia patens*

Malachite
Siproeta stelenes (si-pro-ay-tah • steel-lings)

Family

Nymphalidae (Brushfoots)
(nim-FAL-ah-dee)

Flight period

Southern Florida
All year

Southern Texas
June–March, but they are not
present every year.

Wingspan

2 ¾–3 ⅛ inches

Identification

Dorsal/Upperside

The dorsal/upperside of the forewing and hindwing are dark brown with green spots and patches. The hindwing has a short tail.

Ventral/Underside

The surface markings on the ventral/underside of the forewing and hindwing are the same as the dorsal/upperside, except they are a paler brownish-orange.

Host/Larval Food Plants

Green Shrimp Plant – *Blechum brownei*
Gregg's Tube Tongue – *Justicia pilosella*
Runyon's Water-willow – *Justicia runyonii*
Wild Petunia – *Ruellia* spp.

Mexican Petunia — *Ruellia simplex*

Wild Petunia — *Ruellia humilis*

The Life Cycle

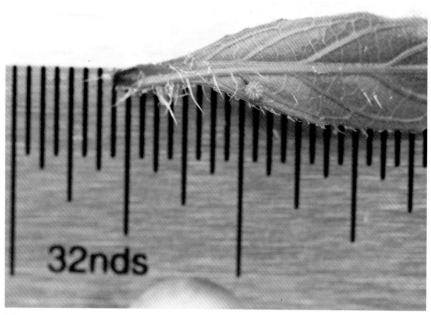

The eggs are green and about 1/32 inch.

The eggs are laid singly, usually on the tops of the leaves or on the stem.

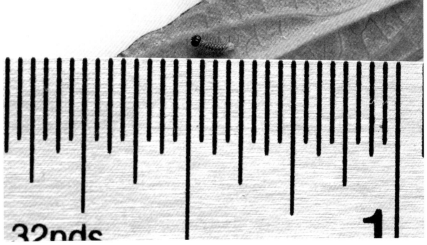

It takes about 4 to 7 days for the egg to hatch. When it hatches, the caterpillar is between ³⁄₃₂ to ⅛ inch long.

The caterpillar's body is blackish. It has branched black tentacles on its head, and its body has rows of long tubercles topped with black spikes.

In the last instar, the caterpillar is about 2 ¼ inches long. The caterpillar stage lasts up to 38 days.

The chrysalis stage can last up to 15 days.

Adult Food

The adults prefer rotting fruit. Occasionally they feed on dung, carrion and nectar from flowers. A couple of their preferred nectar plants are Snow Squarestem and Spanish Needles.

Rotting fruit

Monarch

Danaus plexippus (dan-ay-us • plex-ih-pus)

Family

Nymphalidae (Brushfoots)
(nim-FAL-ah-dee)

Flight period

March–November

Deep South
All year

Wingspan

3½–4 inches

Identification

Dorsal/Upperside

The dorsal/upperside is orange with black veins and a black border that contains two rows of white spots. The forewing has white spots near the apex. The hindwing of the female has thick veins, whereas the hindwing of the male has thin veins with a black scent patch near the inner margin.

Ventral/Underside

The ventral/underside is similar to the dorsal, except it is lighter orange.

Host/Larval Food Plants

Milkweed — *Asclepias* spp.

Butterfly Weed — *Asclepias tuberosa*

Common Milkweed — *Asclepias syriaca*

Swamp Milkweed — *Asclepias incarnata*

The Life Cycle

Monarchs have several broods each year. The eggs are ivory and laid singly under the leaves, on top of the leaves, on tight flower buds and also on the stems.

Here is an egg on the stem of a flower bud.

The egg is about 1⁄32 inch wide.

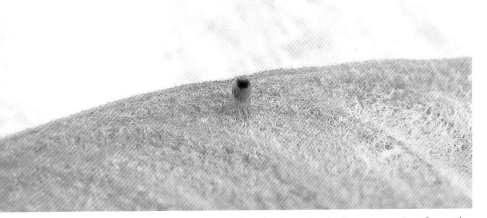

It takes 3 to 6 days for the egg to hatch. One day before emerging from the egg, the caterpillar's black head is visible.

After hatching, the caterpillar will eat most or all of its eggshell.

The caterpillar is about 3/32 inch long after it hatches.

The caterpillars have 5 instars. The one shown above has just finished molting. You can see the head capsule (on the right), which comes off first, and the skin it just crawled out of (on the left). Its antennae are still folded in half, and the new head capsule is light in color. Shortly, the antennae will straighten up and the head capsule will darken. After the caterpillar's new skin dries up, it will turn around and eat its old skin.

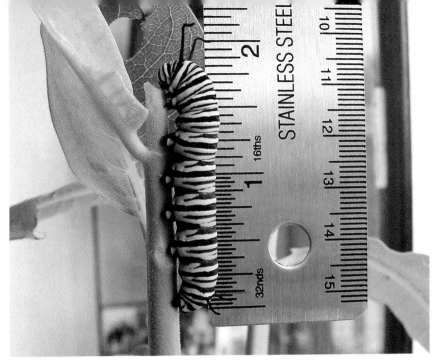

The caterpillar stage lasts for 9 to 16 days. In the last instar, the caterpillar is about 2 inches.

The caterpillar will hang in a J shape for about 24 hours before pupating. Right before it molts for the last time, it will hang straight down. The skin will split behind its head and then the molting begins.

It takes less than 2 minutes to reveal the chrysalis.

As the chrysalis hardens, it becomes smooth and jade green with gold spots. The chrysalis stage lasts for 9 to 14 days. The day before the butterfly emerges, the chrysalis becomes transparent.

About 15 minutes after the butterfly begins to emerge from the chrysalis, the wings are completely expanded. It takes several hours for the wings to harden and dry.

Adult Food

Monarchs feed on Aster, Blazing Star, Bougainvillea, Butterfly Bush, Buttonbush, Clover, Cosmos, Eucalyptus, Garden Phlox, Goldenrod, Golden Dewdrop, Hyssop, Ironweed, Joe-Pye Weed, Lantana, Mexican Plum, Mexican Sunflower, Milkweed, Pentas, Purple Coneflower, Verbena, Thistle and Zinnia.

Mexican Sunflower — *Tithonia rotundifolia*

New England Aster — *Symphyotrichum novae-angliae*

Mourning Cloak

Nymphalis antiopa (nim-fal-iss • an-tee-oh-pa)

Family

Nymphalidae (Brushfoots)
(nim-FAL-ah-dee)

Flight period

March–October

South
All year

Wingspan

3–4 inches

Identification

Dorsal/Upperside

The dorsal/upperside is purplish-black with a broad yellow border and a row of iridescent blue spots just inside of the border.

Ventral/Underside

The ventral/underside is dark brown and bark-like in appearance with a yellowish border.

Host/Larval Food Plants

Elm — *Ulmus* spp.
Hackberry — *Celtis* spp.
Paper Birch — *Betula papyrifera*
Poplar — *Populus* spp.
Sugarberry — *Celtis laevigata*
Willow — *Salix* spp.

Black Willow — *Salix nigra*

The Life Cycle

Mourning Cloaks have 1 or 2 broods each year. The eggs are laid in clusters around twigs and on the leaves of the host plant. They are yellowish-cream with white ridges when first laid. As they develop, they turn red and then black. Each egg is slightly smaller than 1/32 inch wide. It takes 10 to 14 days for the eggs to hatch.

The caterpillars stay together until they are fully grown. At that time, they will leave the host plant in search of a place to make their chrysalises.

The caterpillar stage lasts for 14 to 18 days. In the last instar, the caterpillar is about 2 3/16 inches long.

The chrysalis stage lasts for 8 to 15 days.

The adult overwinters in tree crevices, hollow logs and other sheltered spots. They can be seen on warm, sunny winter days. In the summer, they may aestivate during the hottest months. They can live up to 12 months.

Adult Food

Mourning Cloaks prefer dung, rotting fruit and tree sap, but they also feed on Andromeda Bush, Brazilian Verbena, Butterfly Bush, Cherry Blossoms, Coneflower, Dogbane, Goldenrod, Lantana, Lilac, Manzanita, Milkweed, New Jersey Tea, Pussy Willow Flowers and Shasta Daisy.

Fruit

Painted Lady
Vanessa cardui (van-ess-ah • car-du-i)

Family
Nymphalidae (Brushfoots)
(nim-FAL-ah-dee)

Flight period
May–October

South
All year

Wingspan
1 ¾–2 ½ inches

Identification

Dorsal/Upperside

The dorsal/upperside is mainly orange with black marks and white spots near the apex of the forewing. The hindwing has black marks and three rows of black spots near the outer margin.

Ventral/Underside

The ventral/underside is brown with a cream cobweb pattern. The forewing has pink markings. The hindwing has a row of small blue marks between the margin and the four small eyespots.

Host/Larval Food Plants

Borage — *Borago officinalis*
Hollyhock — *Alcea* spp.
Mallow — *Malva* spp.
Plantain — *Plantago* spp.
Sunflower — *Helianthus* spp.
Thistle — *Cirsium* spp.
Tree Mallow — *Lavatera maritima*

Mallow — *Malva* **spp.**

Thistle — *Cirsium* spp.

The Life Cycle

32nds

Painted Ladies have several broods each year. The eggs are between 1/64 and 1/32 inch wide. They are light green and laid singly. If they are fed instant diet (an artificial food you can purchase), the eggs will be light aqua in color.

It takes between 5 and 9 days for the egg to hatch. The day before the caterpillar hatches, the egg turns dark, revealing the caterpillar.

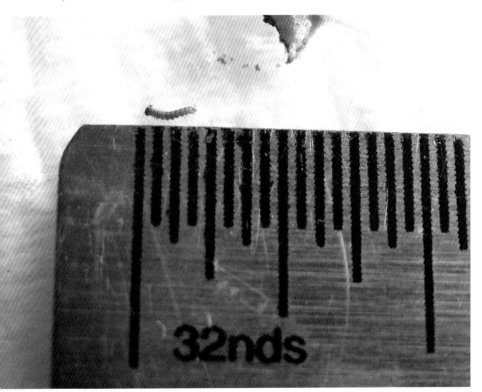

When it hatches, the caterpillar is between 1/16 and 3/32 inch long.

The caterpillar encloses itself in a silken nest in the leaves of the host plant for protection while it eats.

The caterpillar stage lasts for 12 to 18 days. In the last instar, the caterpillar is about 1 ⅝ inches long.

The caterpillar will hang in a J shape for about 24 hours before pupating. It will be in the chrysalis for 9 to 14 days. The day before it emerges, the chrysalis will become transparent.

Adult Food

Some of the flowers that Painted Ladies nectar on include Anchor Plant, Aster, Blazing Star, Brazilian Verbena, Butterfly Bush, Buttonbush, California Buckwheat, Coreopsis, Cosmos, Escallonia, Ironweed, Joe-Pye Weed, Lantana, Mexican Sunflower, Milkweed, New England Aster, Privet, Purple Coneflower, Red Clover, Scabiosa, Scarlet Monkeyflower, Thistle and Zinnia.

Sand Coreopsis — *Coreopsis lanceolata*

Pearl Crescent

Phyciodes tharos (fy-see-oh-dees • thar-ohs)

Family

Nymphalidae (Brushfoots)
(nim-FAL-ah-dee)

Flight period

April–November

Deep South
All year

Wingspan

1 ¼–1 ⅝ inches

Identification

Dorsal/Upperside

The dorsal/upperside is orange with a lace-like pattern made with thin, black lines. The wings have black borders and there's a row of small spots near the border of the hindwing. The female is larger than the male and is darker with white markings on her forewing.

Ventral/Underside

The ventral/underside is mottled with a dark marginal patch consisting of a silvery crescent.

Host/Larval Food Plants

Aster — *Symphyotrichum* spp.

Smooth Blue Aster — *Symphyotrichum laevis*

Heart-Leaved Aster — *Symphyotrichum cordifoium*

New England Aster — *Symphyotrichum novae-angliae*

The Life Cycle

The adult female Pearl Crescent lays her eggs on the underside of the host leaf.

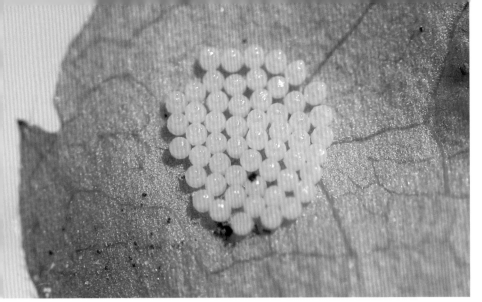

Pearl Crescents have several broods each year. The eggs are pale yellowish-green and laid in small clusters. It takes between 4 and 6 days for the eggs to hatch.

In the last instar, the caterpillar is about ¾ inch long. The caterpillar stage lasts for 10 to 12 days, except for the last brood, which overwinters.

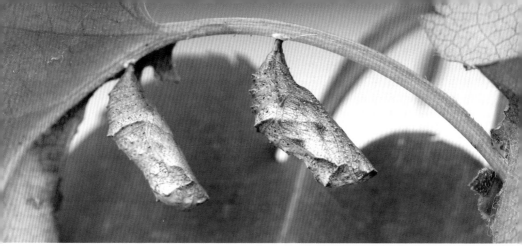

The chrysalis stage lasts for 7 to 12 days.

Adult Food

Some of the flowers that Pearl Crescents nectar on include Aster, Black-Eyed Susan, Butterfly Bush, Butterfly Weed, Dogbane, Frostweed, Joe-Pye Weed, Mexican Sunflower, Milkweed, Obedient Plant, Orange Coneflower, Purple Coneflower, Shepherd's Needle, Snow-on-the-Mountain, Thistle and Winter Cress.

Butterfly Weed — *Asclepias tuberosa*

Queen

Danaus gilippus (dan-ay-us • gil-ih-pus)

Family

Nymphalidae (Brushfoots)
(nim-FAL-ah-dee)

Flight period

April–November

Deep South
All year

Wingspan

2 ⅝–3 ¾ inches

Identification

Dorsal/Upperside

The dorsal/upperside is mahogany with white spots in the black wing margins. The forewing has white spots in the postmedian and subapical. The male has a black scent patch along the inner margin.

Ventral/Underside

The ventral/underside is similar to the dorsal side, except the hindwing has black veins.

Host/Larval Food Plants

Bearded Swallow-Wort — *Cynanchum barbigerum*
Blodgett's Swallow-Wort — *Cynanchum blodgettii*
Climbing Milkweed — *Sarcostemma* spp.
Milkweed — *Asclepias* spp.
White Twinevine — *Sarcostemma clausum*

Tropical Milkweed — *Asclepias curassavica*

The Life Cycle

Queens have several broods each year. The eggs are about 1/32 inch wide. They are white and laid singly on leaves, stems and flower buds.

It takes 4 to 6 days for the egg to hatch.

The caterpillar has three pairs of black filaments. The caterpillar stage lasts for 14 to 16 days. In the last instar, the caterpillar is about 2 inches long.

The chrysalis stage lasts for 9 to 11 days. The color of the chrysalis can be pink or green.

Adult Food

Certain flowers have alkaloids (i.e., chemical compounds) that are required for breeding. The males will seek these out. Some of these are in the genera Ageratum, Eupatorium and Heliotropium.

Some of the flowers that Queens nectar on include Aster, Butterfly Bush, Coneflower, Frogfruit, Ghost Plant, Goldenrod, Gumweed, Heliotrope, Hibiscus, Mexican Sunflower, Milkweed, Mistflower, Pentas, Porterweed, Spanish Needles, St. John's Wort, Starflower, Thistle, Threadleaf Groundsel, Verbena, White Twinevine, Wild Tamarind and Zinnia.

Hibiscus — *Hibiscus* spp.

Question Mark

Polygonia interrogationis (pol-ih-go-nee-ah • in-ter-oh-gat-ee-oh-nis)

Family

Nymphalidae (Brushfoots)
(nim-FAL-ah-dee)

Flight period

April–November

Wingspan

2 ¼–3 inches

Identification

Dorsal/Upperside

The dorsal/upperside of the forewing is orange with brownish-black spots. The Question Mark is similar in appearance to the Eastern Comma, except it has an extra mark above the three spots that are in a row and it is larger. The hindwing of the summer form is mostly black, whereas the hindwing of the winter form is mostly orange.

Ventral/Underside

The ventral/underside looks like a dead leaf. There is a silvery spot on the hindwing that resembles a question mark.

Host/Larval Food Plants

Elm — *Ulmus* spp.
False Nettle — *Boehmeria cylindrica*
Hackberry — *Celtis* spp.
Hops — *Humulus* spp.
Nettle — *Urtica* spp.
Sugarberry — *Celtis laevigata*

Common Hop — *Humulus lupulus*

The Life Cycle

Question Marks have 2 broods each year. The eggs are green and laid singly, in small groups or stacked. They lay their eggs on the host plant, and they also lay them on the ground, on another plant or on an object that is close to the host plant. If the egg is not on the host plant when the caterpillar emerges, the caterpillar seeks it out.

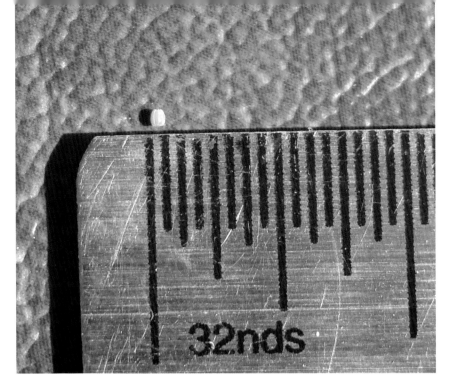

The egg is between 1/64 and 1/32 inch wide.

The egg darkens as the caterpillar develops. It takes 3 to 7 days for the egg to hatch.

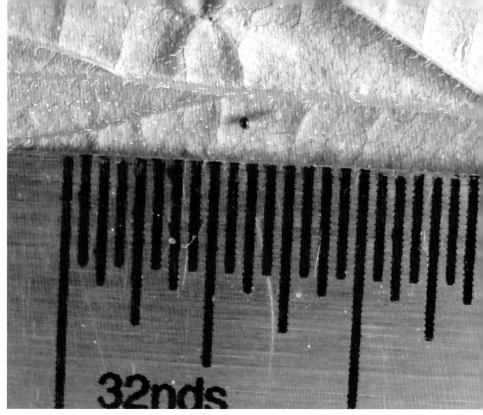

When the egg hatches, the caterpillar is about 1/16 inch long.

The caterpillars can be found underneath the leaves of the host plant.

The caterpillar's appearance can vary.

The caterpillar stage lasts for 14 to 18 days. In the last instar, the caterpillar is about 1 ¾ inches long.

Before it pupates, the caterpillar hangs in a J shape.

This caterpillar is molting for the last time as it reveals its chrysalis. It is in the chrysalis for 7 to 10 days.

The adult can live up to 8 months. It overwinters in hollow logs, wood piles, crevices of trees, earthen crevices, under bark or under shingles.

Adult Food

Question Marks prefer carrion, dung, puddling, rotting fruit and tree sap, but they will also feed on Aster, Butterfly Bush, Purple Coneflower, Milkweed and Sweet Pepperbush.

Purple Coneflower — *Echinacea purpurea*

Rotting fruit

Red Admiral

Vanessa atalanta (van-ess-ah • at-ah-lan-tah)

Family

Nymphalidae (Brushfoots)
(nim-FAL-ah-dee)

Flight period

March–November

Deep South
All year

Wingspan

1 ¾–2 ½ inches

Identification

Dorsal/Upperside

The dorsal/upperside is black. The forewing has reddish-orange bands and small white spots near the apex. The hindwing has a reddish-orange border.

Ventral/Underside

The ventral/underside of the forewing is similar to the dorsal side. The hindwing is mottled and lacks the reddish-orange border.

Host/Larval Food Plants

False Nettle — *Boehmeria cylindrica*
Mamaki — *Pipturus albidus*
Nettle — *Urtica* spp.
Pennsylvania Pellitory — *Parietaria pensylvanica*
Wood Nettle — *Laportea canadensis*

False Nettle — *Boehmeria cylindrica*

The Life Cycle

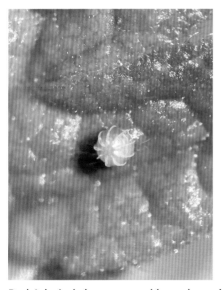 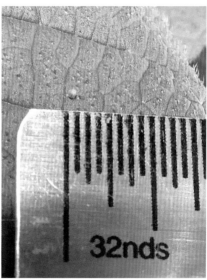

Red Admirals have several broods each year. The eggs are green, laid singly and measure between $\frac{1}{64}$ and $\frac{1}{32}$ inch wide. It takes 3 to 6 days for the egg to hatch.

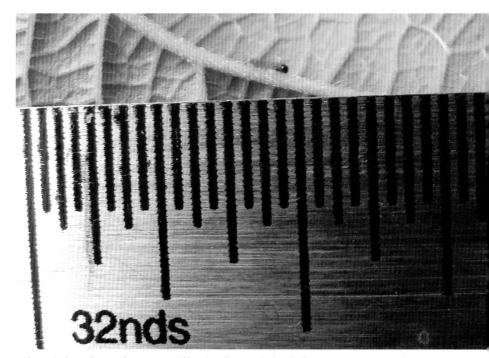

When it hatches, the caterpillar is about $\frac{1}{16}$ inch long. For protection, it stitches its host leaf closed and eats the leaf from within.

The caterpillar stage lasts for 14 to 21 days. In the last instar, the caterpillar is about 1½ inches long.

The caterpillar hangs in a J shape for about 24 hours before pupating.

The chrysalis stage lasts for 8 to 12 days.

The chrysalis becomes transparent the day before the butterfly emerges.

Adult Food

Red Admirals can be found puddling, and they also feed on dung, rotting fruit, salts from human perspiration and tree sap.

Some of the flowers that they nectar on include Alfalfa, Anchor Plant, Aster, Bougainvillea, Brazilian Verbena, Butterfly Bush, Choke Cherry, Purple Coneflower, Crab Apple, Creeping Phlox, Escallonia, Golden Dewdrop, Lantana, Lilac, Milkweed, Pentas, Red Clover, Salvia and Sedum.

Rotting fruit

Purple Coneflower — *Echinacea purpurea*

"Ice Ballet" Swamp Milkweed — *Asclepias incarnata*

Butterfly Weed – *Asclepias tuberosa*

Red-Spotted Purple

Limenitis arthemis (le-men-ee-tis • ar-thee-mis)

Family

Nymphalidae (Brushfoots)
(nim-FAL-ah-dee)

Flight period

April–October

Wingspan

3–3 ½ inches

Identification

Dorsal/Upperside

The dorsal/upperside is mainly purplish-blue with iridescent blue on the outer portion of the hindwing.

Ventral/Underside

The ventral/underside is brownish-black with reddish-orange spots near the base and a row of orange spots near the outer edge.

Host/Larval Food Plants

Apple — *Malus* spp.
Aspen — *Populus* spp.
Basswood — *Tilia* spp.
Birch — *Betula* spp.
Cherry — *Prunus* spp.
Cottonwood — *Populus* spp.
Deerberry — *Vaccinium stamineum*
Hawthorn — *Crataegus* spp.
Hornbeam — *Carpinus caroliniana*
Oak — *Quercus* spp.
Pear — *Pyrus* spp.
Poplar — *Populus* spp.
Shadbush — *Amelanchier* spp.
Willow — *Salix* spp.

Wild Black Cherry — *Prunus serotina*

Corkscrew Willow — *Salix matsudana* **and Pussy Willow** — *Salix discolor*

The Life Cycle

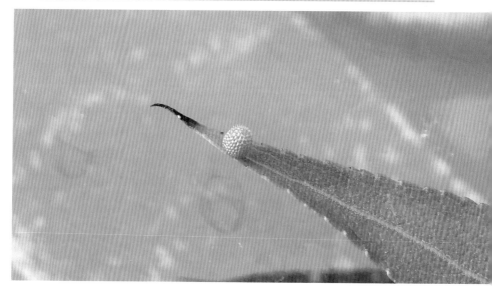

Red-Spotted Purples have 2 broods each year. The eggs are grayish-green and laid singly on the tip of the host leaf.

The egg is about $\frac{1}{32}$ inch wide.

The egg darkens as the caterpillar develops. It takes 4 to 8 days for the egg to hatch.

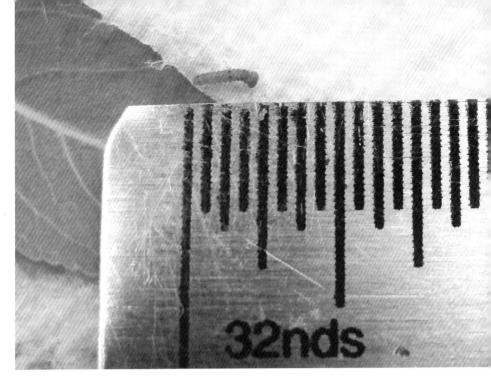

When it hatches, the caterpillar is between 3/32 and 1/8 inch long.

The caterpillar often eats along the vein of the leaf.

This caterpillar has just finished molting. Its old skin is behind it. The new head capsule and spined horns are a light color. Shortly they will darken.

The 3rd instar of the last brood overwinters in a hibernaculum. To make the hibernaculum, it first secures the leaf to the twig with silk. Then it stitches the leaf together with silk and crawls in.

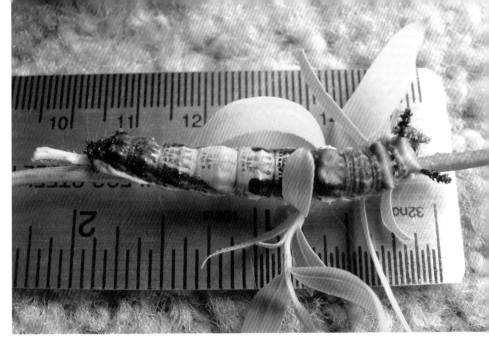

The caterpillar stage lasts for 21 to 28 days, except for the last brood, which overwinters. In the last instar, the caterpillar is about 2 inches long.

The caterpillar will hang in a J shape before pupating.

The chrysalis stage lasts for 6 to 12 days.

Adult Food

Red-Spotted Purples feed on aphid honeydew, carrion, dung, rotting fruit, spittle of spittlebugs on Goldenrods, tree sap, Brazilian Verbena, Butterfly Bush, Dogbane, Lantana, Milkweed, Pentas, Privet, Purple Coneflower, Spiraea, Staghorn, Sumac, Thistle and Viburnum.

Purple Coneflower – *Echinacea purpurea*

"Pink Delight" Butterfly Bush – *Buddleia davidii*

Rotting fruit

Tawny Emperor
Asterocampa clyton (a-ster-cam-pee-ah • cly-ton)

Family

Nymphalidae (Brushfoots)
(nim-FAL-ah-dee)

Flight period

June–August

Deep South
March–November

Wingspan

1 ⅝–2 ¾ inches

Identification

Female

Male

The adult is brown to orangish-brown with two complete dark bars on the dorsal/upperside forewing cell. The dorsal/upperside hindwings are orange with black submarginal spots in one form, and all black in the other form.

Host/Larval Food Plants

Hackberry – *Celtis* spp.

Hackberry — *Celtis occidentalis*

The Life Cycle

The Tawny Emperor has 1 brood in the north from June to August and 3 broods in the south from March to November. The eggs are almost ⅟₃₂ inch and white. They turn darker before hatching. It takes about 8 to 10 days for the eggs to hatch.

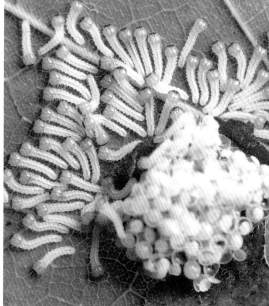

When the caterpillar hatches, it's between ⅟₁₆ and ³⁄₃₂ inch.

The young caterpillars feed in groups. In later instars when feeding, they become solitary.

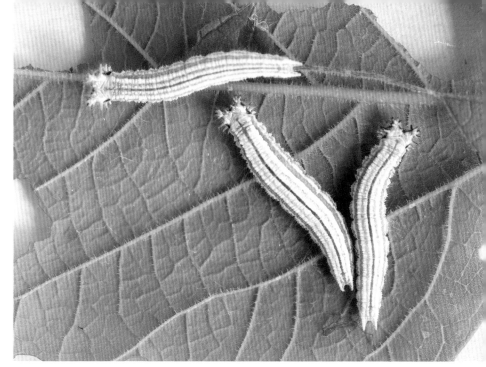

In the last instar, the caterpillar is about 1 9/16 inches long. The body is green with yellow and white longitudinal stripes and a pair of short tails on the posterior end. The head has short spines on the sides and a pair of short, black-tipped horns on top. The caterpillar stage can be as long as a little over 4 weeks.

The chrysalis stage is about 10 to 14 days.

Adult Food

Adults feed on tree sap, rotting fruit, carrion, dung and even moist bread, but almost never on flowers.

Moist bread

Viceroy
Limenitis archippus (le-min-ee-tis • ar-kip-us)

Family

Nymphalidae (Brushfoots)
(nim-FAL-ah-dee)

Flight period

April–October

Florida
All year

Wingspan

2 ½–3 ¼ inches

Identification

Dorsal/Upperside

The dorsal/upperside is orange with black veins and a black border that contains two rows of white spots. The forewing has a black postmedian line and white spots. The hindwing has a black postmedian line.

Ventral/Underside

The ventral/underside is similar to the dorsal side, except it is a lighter orange and has larger white spots.

Host/Larval Food Plants

Aspen — *Populus* spp.
Cottonwood — *Populus* spp.
Poplar — *Populus* spp.
Willow — *Salix* spp.

Cottonwood — *Populus* **spp.**

The Life Cycle

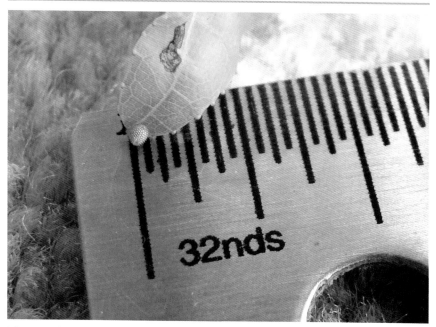

Viceroys have 2 to 3 broods each year. The eggs are grayish-green, about $\frac{1}{32}$ inch wide and usually laid singly on the tip of the host leaf. It takes 4 to 8 days for the egg to hatch.

When it hatches, the caterpillar is about $\frac{3}{32}$ inch long.

Young caterpillars eat along the vein of the leaf. They make a ball with silk, leaf bits and dung, which they hang from the leaf they are eating on. It is believed that this ball may distract predators.

The caterpillar stage lasts for 12 to 18 days, except for the 3rd instar of the last brood, which overwinters in a hibernaculum. In the last instar, the caterpillar is about 2 inches long.

This caterpillar will hang in a J shape as it prepares to pupate.

The chrysalis stage lasts for 8 to 12 days. Before the butterfly emerges, the chrysalis becomes transparent.

About 5 minutes after the Viceroy begins to eclose from the chrysalis, the wings are completely expanded. It takes a few hours for the wings to harden and dry.

Adult Food

Viceroys can be found puddling, and they also feed on aphid honeydew, carrion, decaying fungi, dung, rotting fruit, tree sap, Aster, Black-Eyed Susan, Brazilian Verbena, Butterfly Bush, Canada Thistle, Goldenrod, Hyssop, Joe-Pye Weed, Milkweed, Purple Coneflower, Sedum and Shepherd's Needle.

Rotting fruit

Zebra Heliconian

Heliconius charithonia (hel-ih-co-nee-us • char-ih-tho-nee-ah)

Family

Nymphalidae (Brushfoots)
(nim-FAL-ah-dee)

Flight period

Southern Florida and Texas
All year

North
Warmer months

Wingspan

2 ¾–4 inches

Identification

Dorsal/Upperside

The dorsal/upperside is dark brown with pale yellow stripes. On the marginal and submarginal area, there is a row of pale yellow spots.

Ventral/Underside

The ventral/underside is similar, but lighter. There are red spots near the inner margin.

Host/Larval Food Plants

All Passion-Vine (*Passiflora* spp.), except Red Passion Flower (*Passiflora racemosa* and *Passiflora coccinea*), which is toxic to them and causes death.

Passion-Vine — *Passiflora* spp.

The Life Cycle

Zebra Heliconians have several broods each year. The eggs are orangish-yellow. They lay their eggs singly or in groups on the leaves, leaf buds and tendrils of the host plant. It takes 3 to 6 days for the eggs to hatch.

When the caterpillar hatches, it is about 3/32 inch long.

In the last instar, the caterpillar is about 1 ¾ inches long. The caterpillar stage lasts for 10 to 14 days.

The chrysalis stage lasts for 5 to 12 days.

Adults roost communally every night in the same place.

Adults live up to 7 months. Zebra Heliconians are one of the few butterflies that feed on pollen. It is believed that this is what enables them to live so long.

Adult Food

Some of the flowers that Zebra Heliconians nectar on include African Daisy, Blanket Flower, Blue Plumbago, Bougainvillea, Butterfly Bush, Firebush, Golden Dewdrop, Jatropha, Lantana, Mexican Sunflower, Mistflower, Passion-Vine, Pentas, Porterweed, Red Powder Puff, Sage, Shepherd's Needle, Spanish Needles, Stokes Aster, Thoroughwort, Verbena and Zinnia.

Bougainvillea — *Bougainvillea* spp.

Common Checkered-Skipper

Pyrgus communis (peer-guss • kom-mu-nis)

Family

Hesperiidae (Skippers)
(hes-per-EYE-ah-dee)

Flight period

February–October

Wingspan

¾–1 ¼ inches

Identification

Dorsal/Upperside

The dorsal/upperside of the male is black with numerous small, white spots and bluish-gray on the base of the wings and thorax, whereas the female is brownish-black with fewer white spots.

Ventral/Underside

The ventral/underside is white with tan or olive irregular bands.

Host/Larval Food Plants

Globemallows — *Sphaeralcea* spp.

Hollyhock — *Alcea* spp.

Mallow — *Malva* spp.

Sida — *Sida* spp.

Threelobe False Mallow — *Malvastrum coromandelianum*

Velvetleaf — *Abutilon theophrasti*

Hollyhock — *Alcea* spp.

Mallow — *Malva* spp.

The Life Cycle

Common Checkered-Skippers have 2 to 3 broods each year. The eggs are laid singly on leaf buds, stems, tops or bottoms of leaves. It takes 4 to 8 days for the eggs to hatch.

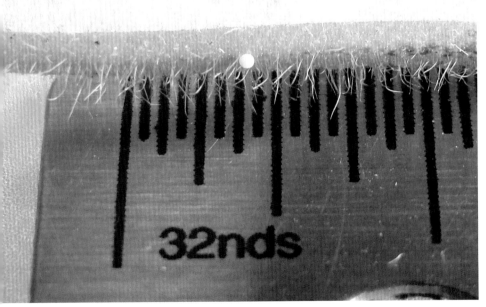

The egg is greenish-white and about 1/64 inch wide.

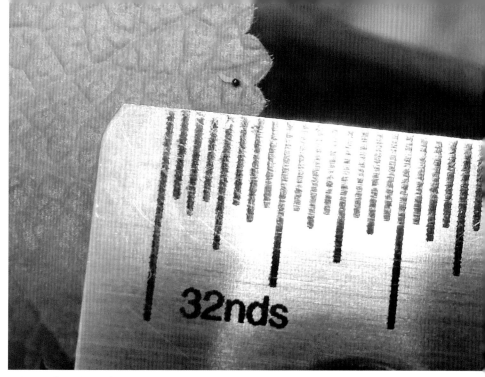

When it hatches, the caterpillar is about 1/16 inch long. They live inside folded leaves, which they stitch together with silk.

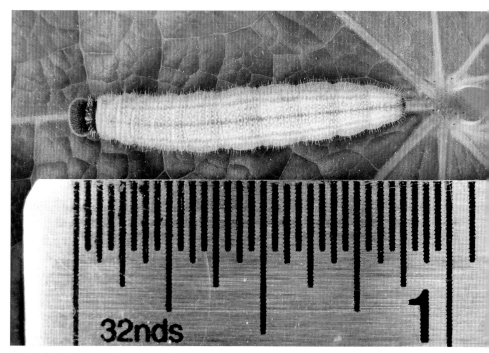

In the last instar, the caterpillar is about 7/8 inch long.

Before pupating, the caterpillar's back turns pinkish. The caterpillar stage lasts for 22 to 30 days, except for the last brood, which overwinters in the last instar.

They pupate within a leaf, which they stitch together with silk. The chrysalis stage lasts for 7 to 14 days.

The chrysalis becomes transparent before the butterfly emerges.

Adult Food

Common Checkered-Skippers can be found puddling, and they also feed on Aster, Beggar's Ticks, Blue Mistflower, Bluets, Brazilian Verbena, Catclaw Mimosa, Dandelion, Dewberry, Fleabane, Frogfruit, Golden Crownbeard, Indian Blanket, Knapweed, Marigold, Milkweed, Monarda, New England Aster, New Jersey Tea, Pearly Everlasting, Red Clover, Shepherd's Needles, Spring Beauty, Thistle, Thoroughwort and Violets.

Silver-Spotted Skipper
Epargyreus clarus (eh-par-jy-ree-us • clar-us)

Family
Hesperiidae (Skippers)
(hes-per-EYE-ah-dee)

Flight period
May–October

Deep South
February–December

Wingspan
1 ¾–2 ⅝ inches

Identification

Dorsal/Upperside

The dorsal/upperside is brown with a checkered wing fringe. The forewing has gold spots across the median. The hindwing is lobed.

Ventral/Underside

The ventral/underside is similar to the dorsal side, with a large silver-white patch in the median of the hindwing.

Host/Larval Food Plants

Black Locust — *Robinia pseudoacacia*
Butterfly Pea — *Clitoria mariana*
Deerweed — *Lotus scoparius*
Downy Milkpea — *Galactia volubilis*
False Indigo — *Amorpha* spp.
Hog-Peanut — *Amphicarpaea bracteata*
Honey Locust — *Gleditsia triacanthos*
Hyacinth Bean — *Lablab purpureus*
Lead Plant — *Amorpha* spp.
Tick-Trefoil — *Desmodium* spp.
Wisteria — *Wisteria* spp.

Wisteria — *Wisteria* **spp.**

The Life Cycle

Silver-Spotted Skippers have 2 to 4 broods each year. The eggs are laid singly on the leaves and stems of the host plant. They are also laid on things close to the host plant. When that happens, the caterpillar must seek it out.

When first laid, the egg is a light turquoise-green. As the caterpillar develops, the egg will form a red ring around it and a red spot on top. Before hatching, the caterpillar's head will become visible.

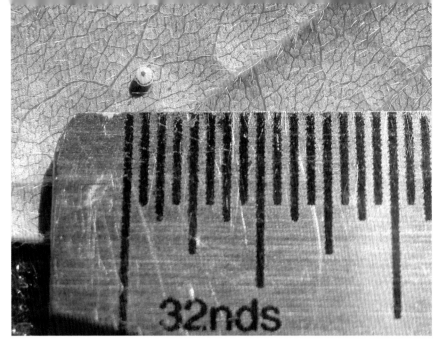

The egg is about ¹⁄₃₂ inch wide. It takes 4 to 8 days for the egg to hatch.

When it hatches, the caterpillar is about ³⁄₃₂ inch long.

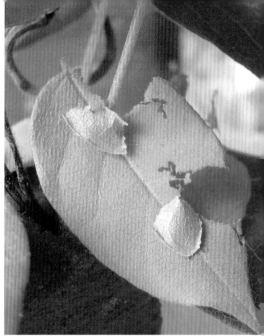

Young caterpillars cut and fold sections of leaves to create shelters. Older ones live in whole leaves that they've silked together. They stay in these leaf shelters when not eating.

In the last instar, the caterpillar is about 1⅜ inches long. The caterpillar stage lasts for 24 to 30 days.

The chrysalis stage lasts for 5 to 14 days, except for the last brood, which overwinters.

Adult Food

Silver-Spotted Skippers can be found puddling, and they also feed on Alfalfa, Black-Eyed Susan, Blazing Star, Butterfly Bush, Buttonbush, Dogbane, Goldenrod, Indigo, Ironweed, Joe-Pye Weed, Mexican Sunflower, Milkweed, Monarda, New Jersey Tea, Perennial Pea, Purple Coneflower, Red Clover, Thistle, Vetch and Wild Sweet William.

Wild Blue Indigo — *Baptisia australis*

Wild Indigo Duskywing

Erynnis baptisiae (ee-ry-en-iss • bap-tee-sy-ee)

Family

Hesperiidae (Skippers)
(hes-per-EYE-ah-dee)

Flight period

April–October

Wingspan

¾–1 ¼ inches

Identification

Dorsal/Upperside

The dorsal/upperside of the male is dark brown with several pale brown spots. The forewing is darker at the base and has glassy white spots near the apex and a reddish-brown patch at the end of the cell. The hindwing has a pale cell-end bar and pale spots. The female is similar but lighter and has a sharper pattern and larger glassy white spots.

Ventral/Underside

The ventral/underside is dark brown and has two rows of pale marginal spots.

Host/Larval Food Plants

Canadian Milkvetch — *Astragalus canadensis*
Crown Vetch — *Securigera varia*
False Lupine — *Thermopsis villosa*
Indigo — *Baptisia* spp.
Lupine — *Lupinus* spp.

Yellow Wild Indigo — *Baptisia tinctoria*

The Life Cycle

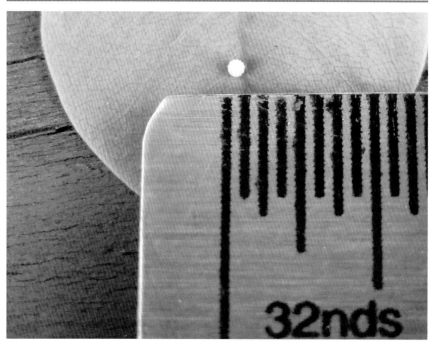

Wild Indigo Duskywings have 2 broods each year. The egg is creamy white, between ⅟₆₄ and ⅟₃₂ inch wide and laid singly on the host leaf.

It takes 4 to 6 days for the egg to hatch. As the caterpillar begins to develop, the egg turns orange. Shortly before the caterpillar ecloses from the egg, the egg darkens.

When it hatches, the caterpillar is about ⅟₁₆ inch long. The caterpillar constructs a silken leaf shelter to which it retires when not eating.

In the last instar, the caterpillar is about 1³⁄₁₆ inches long. The caterpillar stage of the 1st brood lasts for 12 to 24 days. The caterpillars of the 2nd brood overwinter in the last instar.

They pupate within a silken leaf shelter.

As the chrysalis hardens it turns dark. The chrysalis stage lasts for 8 to 20 days.

Adult Food

Wild Indigo Duskywings can be found puddling, and they also feed on Aster, Black-Eyed Susan, Blazing Star, Brazilian Verbena, Butterfly Bush, Buttonbush, Clover, Dogbane, Monarda, Purple Coneflower, Sunflower, Wild Geranium, Wild Strawberry, Thistle and Zinnia.

Puddling

Calleta Moth

Eupackardia calleta (you-pack-are-dee-ah • kah-lee-tah)

Family

Saturniidae (Silk Moths)
(sat-uhr-NYE-ah-dee)

Flight period

Southeastern mountains of Arizona
July–August

Central Arizona to Mexico
October–January

Southern Texas
September–November and March–April

Wingspan

3 1/8–4 5/16 inches

Identification

Dorsal/Upperside

The adult's body is black with a red collar and red on the rear of the thorax. The wings are black with conspicuous white postmedian lines, which are wider in females. Triangular white spots on the wings range from large to almost absent.

Ventral/Underside

The ventral/underside is similar to the dorsal.

Host/Larval Food Plants

Ash — *Fraxinus* spp.
Cherry — *Prunus* spp.
Common Lilac — *Syringa vulgaris*
Mexican Jumping Bean — *Sapium biloculare*
Ocotillo — *Fouquieria splendens*
Privet — *Ligustrum* spp.
Texas Sage — *Leucophyllum frutescens*
Willow — *Salix* spp.

Texas Sage — *Leucophyllum frutescens*

The Life Cycle

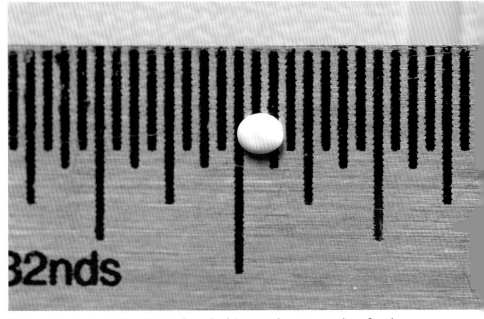

The eggs are about ¹⁄₁₆ to ³⁄₃₂ inch and white. It takes 9 to 12 days for the egg to hatch.

When the caterpillar hatches, it is about ⁵⁄₃₂ to ³⁄₁₆ inch long.

In the last instar, the caterpillar is about 2 15/16 inches long. The caterpillar stage lasts 27 to 34 days.

The cocoon is attached to a twig by a short silken loop and is usually spun near the ground and often in shade. Calleta Moths can take up to two years to emerge from their cocoons.

Adult Food

The adults do not feed because they have no proboscises. For that reason, their lifespan is short, usually a week or less.

Cecropia Moth

Hyalophora cecropia (hy-ah-loaf-oh-rah • see-kroh-pee-ah)

Family

Saturniidae (Silk Moths)
(sat-uhr-NYE-ah-dee)

Flight period

North
May–July

South
March–May

Wingspan

4 5/16–5 7/8 inches

Identification

Dorsal/Upperside

The dorsal/upperside is dark brown with white hair-like scales that create a frosted appearance. The forewing is red at the base and has a red median line. The hindwing has a red and tan postmedian line. Both wings are tan to brown in color along the outer margin and have a crescent spot that is white to a solid rust red.

Ventral/Underside

The ventral/underside is similar to the dorsal side. The body is red with a white collar and white bands on the abdomen. The male has larger antennae and a smaller abdomen.

Host/Larval Food Plants

Alder — *Betula* spp.

Apple — *Malus* spp.

Birch — *Betula* spp.

Box Elder — *Acer negundo*

Cherry — *Prunus* spp.

Dogwood — *Cornus* spp.

Lilac — *Syringa* spp.

Maple — *Acer* spp.

Pear — *Pyrus* spp.

Plum — *Prunus* spp.

Wax Myrtle — *Myrica cerifera*

Willow — *Salix* spp.

Common Lilac — *Syringa vulgaris*

The Life Cycle

Cecropias have 1 brood each year. The eggs are light tan to brown in color. They are laid on both surfaces of the leaf in rows of 2 to 6.

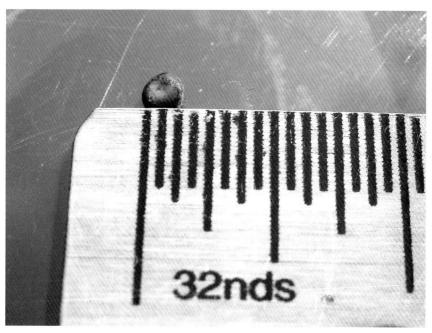

The egg is slightly larger than $\frac{1}{16}$ inch. It takes 10 to 14 days for the egg to hatch.

When it hatches, the caterpillar is about 1/8 inch long. The young caterpillars feed in groups. By the 3rd instar they become solitary.

In the last instar, the caterpillar is about 3 $\frac{15}{16}$ inches long. The caterpillar stage lasts for 37 to 52 days.

The caterpillar makes a cocoon to pupate in. It often spins a cocoon at the base of a bush under thick growth.

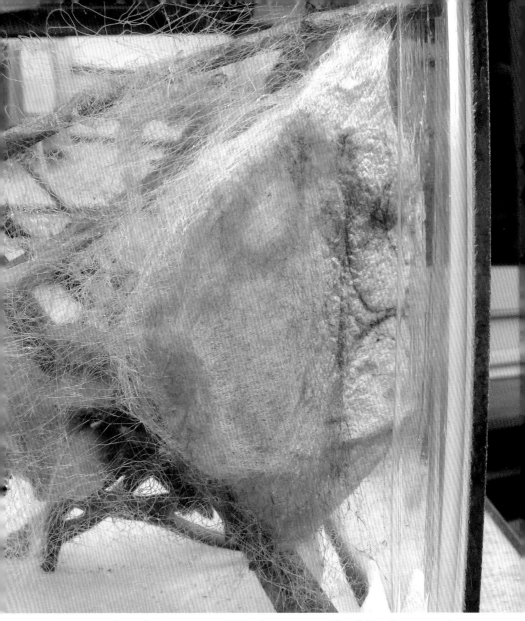

They overwinter in the pupa, within the cocoon. The following year, they eclose from the pupa usually in midmorning.

Adult Food

The adults do not feed because they have no proboscises. For that reason, they are short-lived.

Io Moth

Automeris io (auto-toe-mere-us • i-o)

Family

Saturniidae (Silk Moths)
(sat-uhr-NYE-ah-dee)

Flight period

May–September

Wingspan

2–3 ⅛ inches

Identification

Female

The adults have large eyespots in the middle of their hindwings. There is a thin black line along the sides and bottom of the eyespot and a thicker red line below that.

The female is rusty red to brown.

Male

The male is yellow to tawny or orangish-brown.

Host/Larval Food Plants

Alder — *Betula* spp.
Aspen — *Populus* spp.
Azalea — *Rhododendron* spp.
Basswood — *Tilia* spp.
Bayberry — *Myrica* spp.
Birch — *Betula* spp.
Blackberry — *Rubus* spp.
Box Elder — *Acer negundo*
Cherry — *Prunus* spp.
Clover — *Trifolium* spp.
Corn — *Zea mays*
Cotton — *Gossypium* spp.
Currant — *Ribes* spp.
Deerberry — *Vaccinium stamineum*
Dwarf Poinciana — *Caesalpinia pulcherrima*
Elm — *Ulmus* spp.
Florida Fishpoison Tree — *Piscidia piscipula*
Hackberry — *Celtis* spp.
Hibiscus — *Hibisceae* spp.

Hickory — *Carya* spp.
Maple — *Acer* spp.
Mesquite — *Prosopis* spp.
Nettletree — *Trema micrantha*
Oak — *Quercus* spp.
Palm — *Arecaceae* spp.
Pear — *Pyrus* spp.
Poplar — *Populus* spp.
Raspberry — *Rubus* spp.
Redbay — *Persea borbonia*
Redbud — *Cercis* spp.
Red Mangrove — *Rhizophora mangle*
Rose — *Rosa* spp.
Royal Poinciana — *Delonix regia*
Sassafras — *Sassafras albidum*
Washington Fan Palm — *Washingtonia robusta*
Wax Myrtle — *Myrica* spp.
Willow — *Salix* spp.
Wisteria — *Wisteria* spp.

Hackberry — *Celtis occidentalis*

The Life Cycle

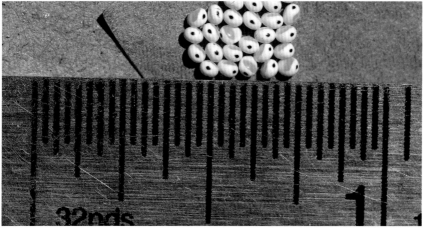

The eggs are white and about ⅟₁₆ inch. When they are first laid, there is a yellow spot on the top of each egg (the opening through which sperm enters). After 3 to 5 days, the spot turns black in the fertilized eggs. As the eggs mature, the yellow areas become orange or brown. It takes about 8 to 18 days for the eggs to hatch.

When the caterpillar emerges, it is about ⅛ inch long and reddish-brown. The young caterpillars feed in groups and walk in a line when moving from place to place. In later instars when feeding, they become solitary. As they get older, they become more yellowish-brown.

When the caterpillars are fully grown, they are green with a white stripe along the body that is edged with a red stripe on the top and a thin red stripe on the bottom. In the last instar, the caterpillar is about 2 ⅜ inches long. The caterpillar stage lasts about 39 to 65 days.

Caution: Caterpillars may cause a stinging sensation if handled.

They spin their cocoons in leaves. The caterpillar is in the cocoon for about 26 to 29 days, except for the last brood, which overwinters. The moth usually emerges in late morning or early afternoon.

Adult Food

The adults do not feed because they have no proboscises. Their lifespan is short, usually a week or less.

Luna Moth

Actias luna (ak-tee-as • loo-na)

Family

Saturniidae (Silk Moths)
(sat-uhr-NYE-ah-dee)

Flight period

North
May–July

South
March–September

Wingspan

3–4 inches

Identification

Dorsal/Upperside

The dorsal/upperside is pale green. Each wing has a transparent eyespot. The hindwings have long, sweeping tails. The outer wing margins of the spring brood are generally reddish-purple. The outer wing margins of later generations are usually yellow. The male has larger antennae and a smaller abdomen.

Ventral/Underside

The ventral/underside is pale green. Each wing has a light-brown zigzag pattern along the submarginal line.

Host/Larval Food Plants

Hickory — *Carya* spp.
Persimmon — *Diospyros virginiana*
Sumac — *Rhus* spp.
Sweetgum — *Liquidambar styraciflua*
Walnut — *Juglans* spp.
White Birch — *Betula papyrifera*

Sweetgum — *Liquidambar styraciflua*

The Life Cycle

Lunas have 1 brood in the north and 3 broods in the south each year. The eggs are white and covered in a mottled-brown adhesive. They are laid on both surfaces of the leaf.

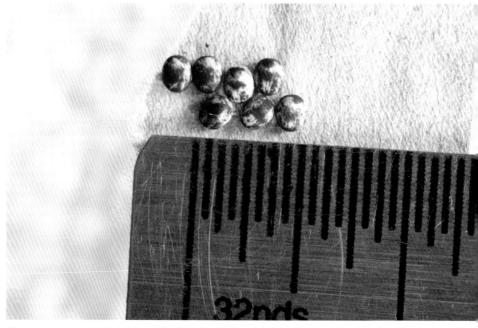

The egg is about 1/16 inch wide. It takes 10 to 16 days for the egg to hatch.

When it hatches, the caterpillar is between ⁵⁄₃₂ and ³⁄₁₆ inch long. They are solitary feeders.

They have 5 instars.

This caterpillar is feeding on Walnut.

In the last instar, the caterpillar is about 2 ⅝ inches long. The caterpillar stage lasts for 38 to 49 days. They turn pale yellow, pale orange or pale green before pupating.

The caterpillar makes a cocoon to pupate in. It spins the cocoon in the leaves of the host plant.

The last brood overwinters in the cocoon. The moth usually emerges in the morning.

Adult Food

The adults do not feed because they have no proboscises. Their lifespan is short, usually a week or less.

Pink-striped Oakworm

Anisota virginiensis (an-eye-soh-tuh • ver-jin-ee-in-sis)

Identification

Female

Females are larger than males. The dorsal/upperside of the female is orangish, and the margins of the wings are purplish. The dorsal/upperside of the male is dark brown and has a large translucent spot on the forewing. Both sexes have a small white spot on each forewing.

Host/Larval Food Plants

Oak — *Quercus* spp.

Chinquapin Oak — *Quercus muehlenbergii*

The Life Cycle

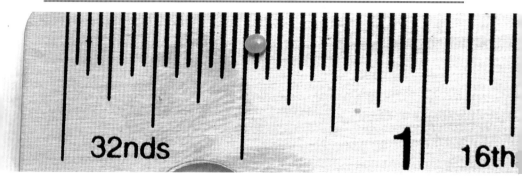

The eggs are a yellowish-orange and between 1/32 and 1/16 inch.

The Pink-striped Oakworm moth lays the eggs in groups on the undersides of leaves.

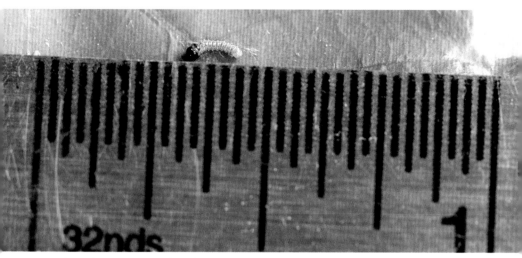

It takes about 11 to 14 days for the eggs to hatch. When it hatches, the caterpillar is about 1/8 inch long.

When the caterpillars are young, they feed together in groups.

In the last instar the caterpillars are about 2 5/16 inches long. The caterpillar stage can last up to 42 days.

The pupa is about ¾ inch long. They overwinter as pupae in the soil.

Adult Food

The adults do not feed because they have no proboscises. Their lifespan is short, usually a week or less.

Polyphemus Moth

Antheraea polyphemus (an-ther-ee-ah • pol-ee-fee-mus)

Family

Saturniidae (Silk Moths)
(sat-uhr-NYE-ah-dee)

Flight period

May–August

Deep South
Most of the year

Wingspan

3 ¹⁵⁄₁₆–5 ¹⁵⁄₁₆ inches

Identification

Dorsal/Upperside

Adults are generally light brown with eyespots on the forewing and hindwing. The dorsal/upperside can have varying degrees of pink and black scaling. The male has larger antennae and a smaller abdomen.

Ventral/Underside

The ventral/underside is generally brown, with varying shades of brown along the marginal line, submarginal line, postmedian line and median line.

Host/Larval Food Plants

Birch — *Betula* spp.
Maple — *Acer* spp.
Oak — *Quercus* spp.
Willow — *Salix* spp.

Chinquapin Oak — *Quercus muehlenbergii*

The Life Cycle

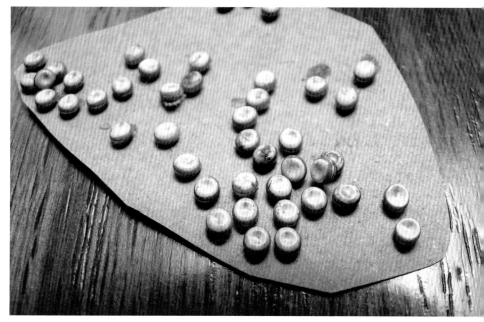

Polyphemuses have several broods each year. The eggs are off-white with two brown bands around the circumference. They are laid on the leaves of host plants.

The egg is slightly wider than 1/16 inch. It takes 8 to 16 days for the egg to hatch.

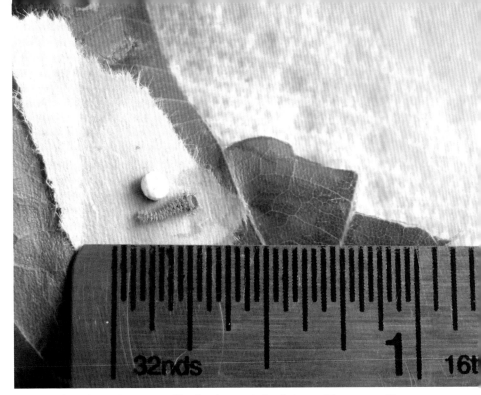

When it hatches, the caterpillar is about 7/32 inch long. The caterpillars are solitary feeders.

There is a brownish V shape on the posterior end of the caterpillar.

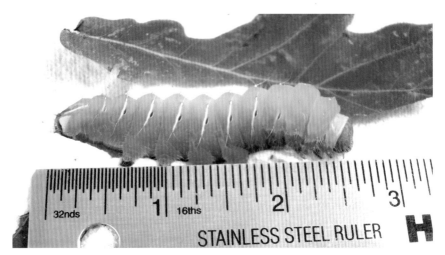

In the last instar, the caterpillar is between 2⅜ and 3¹⁵⁄₁₆ inches long. The caterpillar stage lasts for 39 to 51 days.

The cocoon is usually made with the leaves of the host plant, but sometimes it is made with grass at the base of the host plant. The cocoon is about 1½ inches long. The last brood overwinters in the pupa, within the cocoon. The following year, the moth usually ecloses from the pupa in the afternoon.

For large silk moths (such as Cecropia, Luna and Polyphemus), make a mating cage with ½-inch hardware cloth fencing and place the female inside. The cage can be hung on a shepherd's hook. During the night, the female will release pheromones to attract a male. Mating will continue throughout the day and they will separate at dusk. When they separate, place the female inside a paper bag, where she will lay eggs.

Adult Food

The adults do not feed because they have no proboscises. Their lifespan is short, usually a week or less.

Promethea Moth

Callosamia promethea (cal-oh-sam-ee-ah • pro-me-thee-ah)

Family

Saturniidae (Silk Moths)
(sat-uhr-NYE-ah-dee)

Flight period

North
May–July

South
March–August

Wingspan

2 $^{15}/_{16}$–3 ¾ inches

Identification

Dorsal/Upperside

The dorsal/upperside of the male's wings are dark brown to black with tan borders and light tan postmedian lines. There is pink near the eyespot on the forewing tip. The male has larger antennae and a smaller body. The female's wings are dark brown to reddish-brown with tan postmedian lines and tan spots. The female also has an eyespot on the forewing tip.

Ventral/Underside

The ventral/underside has varying shades of brown from the outer margin to the basal area.

Host/Larval Food Plants

Buttonbush — *Cephalanthus occidentalis*
Cherry — *Prunus* spp.
Common Lilac — *Syringa vulgaris*
Sassafras — *Sassafras albidum*
Spicebush — *Lindera benzoin*
Sweetbay — *Magnolia virginiana*
Sweetgum — *Liquidambar styraciflua*
Tulip Tree — *Liriodendron tulipifera*
White Ash — *Fraxinus americana*

Spicebush — *Lindera benzoin*

The Life Cycle

Prometheae have 2 broods each year. The eggs are whitish and between 1/32 and 1/16 inch wide. They are secured on the host plant leaves with a tan-colored substance. It takes 9 to 16 days for the eggs to hatch.

When they hatch, the caterpillars are between 1/8 and 5/32 inch long.

The young caterpillars feed in groups.

In later instars, they become solitary. With each instar, their appearance changes.

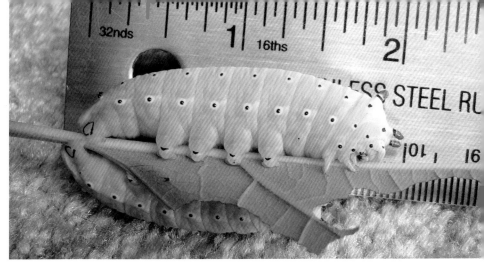

In the last instar, the caterpillar is about 2 inches long.

The caterpillar spins a cocoon in the leaf of the host plant, which it has securely attached to the petiole of the plant with silk. The last brood over-winters in the cocoon.

Adult Food

The adults do not feed because they have no proboscises. For that reason, they have short lifespans.

Rosy Maple Moth

Dryocampa rubicunda (dry-oh-camp-ah • roo-bih-cun-da)

Family

Saturniidae (Silk Moths)
(sat-uhr-NYE-ah-dee)

Flight period

North
May–August

South
April–September

Wingspan

1 5/16–2 1/16 inches

Identification

Dorsal/Upperside

The dorsal/upperside of the body and wings can vary from bright yellow to cream to white. Bright pink usually covers all the wing area, except for the median of the forewing. The hindwing has a wide outer border that is bright pink.

Ventral/Underside

The ventral/underside of the body and wings can vary from bright yellow to cream to white. The wings have pale pink areas. The abdomen has pink stripes and the legs are pink. When handled, they play dead.

Host/Larval Food Plants

Red Maple — *Acer rubrum*
Silver Maple — *Acer saccharinum*
Sugar Maple — *Acer saccharum*
Turkey Oak — *Quercus laevis*

Silver Maple — *Acer saccharinum*

The Life Cycle

Rosy Maple Moths have 1 brood in the north and 2 to 3 broods in the south each year. The eggs are yellow and laid on the leaves of the host plant.

An egg is between 1/32 and 1/16 inch wide. It takes about 10 to 15 days for the egg to hatch. The development of the caterpillar is visible through the egg.

When the caterpillar hatches, it is about 3/32 inch long.

The young caterpillars feed in groups.

In later instars, they become solitary. The caterpillar is about 2 inches long in the last instar.

The caterpillar burrows into the ground to pupate. It does not spin a cocoon. The last brood overwinters in the ground and emerges the following year.

Adult Food

The adults do not feed because they have no proboscises. For that reason, they have short lifespans.

Hummingbird Clearwing

Hemaris thysbe (hem-ah-ris • thiz-bee)

Family

Sphingidae (Sphinx Moths)
(SFEN-jah-dee)

Flight period

March–October

Wingspan

1½–2³⁄₁₆ inches

Identification

Dorsal/Upperside

The dorsal/upperside of the thorax is olive or golden olive and the abdomen is reddish-brown. The forewing cell is either covered or has a bisecting line. Both the forewing and the hindwing have unscaled areas with reddish-brown borders.

Ventral/Underside

The ventral/underside is similar to the dorsal side, except the thorax is pale yellow. The legs are yellowish or pale-colored.

Host/Larval Food Plants

Blueberry — *Vaccinium* spp.
Cranberry — *Vaccinium* spp.
Viburnum — *Viburnum* spp. (used most frequently)

There have been reports that they also use Honeysuckle (*Lonicera* spp.) and Snowberry (*Symphoricarpos* spp.); however, the Hummingbird Clearwing may have been confused with the Snowberry Clearwing.

Old records show that they use Cherry (*Prunus* spp.) and Hawthorn (*Crataegus* spp.), but this needs further investigation.

Arrowwood Viburnum — *Viburnum dentatum*

The Life Cycle

Hummingbird Clearwings have several broods each year. The egg is light green and slightly wider than $\frac{1}{32}$ inch. They are laid on the top or bottom of the host plant leaf, both singly and in pairs. It takes 4 to 6 days for the egg to hatch.

When it hatches, the caterpillar is about $\frac{5}{32}$ inch long.

The caterpillar stage lasts for 10 to 14 days. In the last instar, the caterpillar is about 1 15/16 inches long.

Before making the pupa, the caterpillar's back turns purplish.

It makes a cocoon of silk and debris on the ground, which it pupates in. The pupa stage lasts for 14 to 20 days, except for the last brood, which overwinters.

This shows the expansion of the wings after the moth ecloses from the pupa.

Adult Food

Adult Hummingbird Clearwings are diurnal and can be seen nectaring during the day. Some of the flowers they nectar on include Blackberry Blossoms, Blazing Star, Brazilian Verbena, Butterfly Bush, Buttonbush, Dogbane, Dogwood Blossoms, English Bluebell, Joe-Pye Weed, Lantana, Lilac, Mexican Sunflower, Milkweed, Million Bells, Mint, Monarda, Petunias, Phlox, Purple Coneflower, Thistle and Zinnia.

Snowberry Clearwing

Hemaris diffinis (hem-ah-ris • dif-fin-eyes)

Family

Sphingidae (Sphinx Moths)
(SFEN-jah-dee)

Flight period

March–September

Wingspan

1 3/8–2 inches

Identification

Adult

The adult's body is golden yellow, and the abdomen has black and yellow bands. It has a black band that crosses the eye and goes down the side of the thorax. The legs are black.

Host/Larval Food Plants

Dogbane — *Apocynum* spp.
Honeysuckle — *Lonicera* spp.
Snowberry — *Symphoricarpos* spp.

Creeping Snowberry — *Symphoricarpos mollis*

The Life Cycle

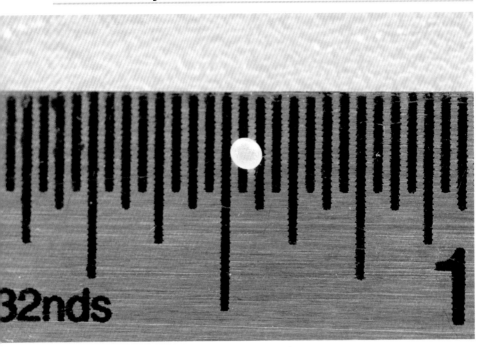

The egg is between 1/32 and 3/64 inch and light green.

It takes about 4 to 7 days for the egg to hatch.

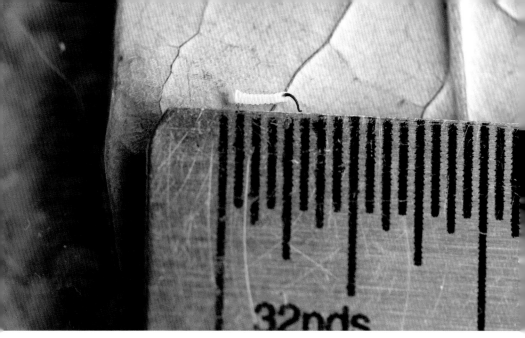

When the caterpillar hatches, it is about 3/32 to 1/8 inch.

When the caterpillar is young, it is usually green with a bluish back and black spots around the spiracles, but sometimes it is brown. It has a horn at the end of the body that is black with a yellow base.

In the last instar, the caterpillar is about 1 ¾ inches long. Right before it gets ready to pupate, its back turns darkish. The caterpillar stage lasts about 18 to 23 days.

32nds   1   16ths

The pupa is about 1 inch. The first brood makes a cocoon with leaf litter on the ground. The last brood overwinters as a pupa in the soil.

Adult Food

Some of the flowers the adult moth feeds on are Autumn Sage, Bee Balm, Canada Violet, Dwarf Bush Honeysuckle, Four O'Clock, Garden Phlox, Hyssop, Lantana, Lilac, Orange Hawkweed, Petunia, Snowberry and Thistle.

Wild Bergamot — *Monarda fistulosa*

Tersa Sphinx

Xylophanes tersa (zi-lo-fanes • ter-sa)

Family

Sphingidae (Sphinx Moths)
(SFEN-jah-dee)

Flight period

May–October

Deep South
All year

Wingspan

2 ⅜–3 ⅛ inches

Identification

Dorsal/Upperside

The female and male are very similar in color. The female's abdomen is fatter. The adult's dorsal/upperside forewing is pale brown with dark brown and whitish lines. The dorsal/upperside hindwing is dark brown with pale yellow markings.

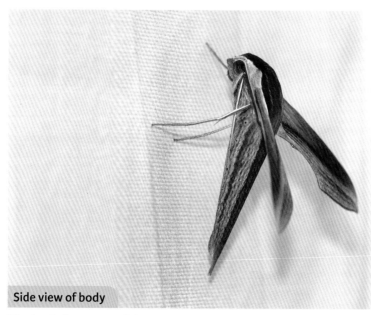

Side view of body

The body is an orangish-tan.

Host/Larval Food Plants

Borreria spp.
Catalpa — *Catalpa bignonioides*
Firebush — *Hamelia patens*
Manettia spp.
Smooth Buttonplant — *Spermacoce glabra*
Starclusters — *Pentas* spp.
Virginia Buttonweed — *Diodia virginiana*

Egyptian Starcluster — *Pentas lanceolata*

The Life Cycle

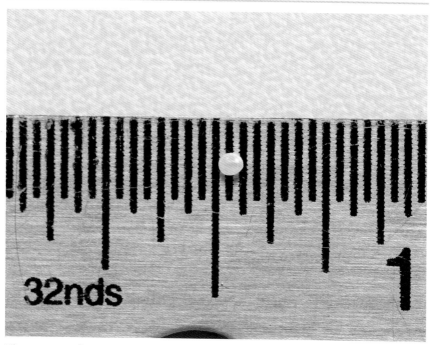

The eggs are between 1/32 and 3/64 inch and pale green.

It takes about 4 to 7 days for the egg to hatch.

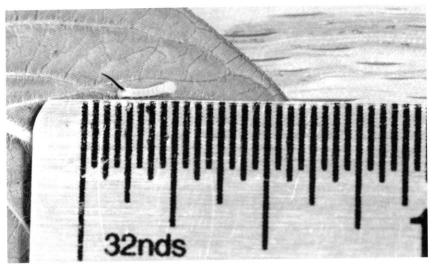

When the caterpillar hatches, it is about ⁵⁄₃₂ inch.

When it gets older, the caterpillar develops one large eyespot and six smaller eyespots along each side.

The caterpillar is generally green or brown. In the last instar, the caterpillar is about 2 ¾ inches long. The caterpillar stage lasts about 18 to 39 days.

They will often use dried leaves to spin into their loosely spun silken cocoon. The cocoon is on the soil surface or just under it. The last brood overwinters in a cocoon and emerges the following year.

Adult Food

Some of the plants that the Tersa Sphinx feeds on are Egyptian Starcluster, Four O'Clock, Honeysuckle and Periwinkle.

Egyptian Starcluster — *Pentas lanceolata*

Giant Leopard Moth

Hypercompe scribonia (hyper-com-pah • scruh-boh-nee-ah)

Family

Arctiidae (Tiger Moths)
(ark-TEE-ah-day)

Flight period

March–November

Wingspan

1 ⅜–2 inches

Identification

Dorsal/Upperside

Dorsal/Upperside

The adult's thorax is white with solid or hollow black spots (or sometimes bluish). The dorsal/upperside forewings may have black spots that are solid or hollow. The spots on the costal margin tend to be solid. The hindwing has black shading along the inner margin and black spots near the apex. As the adults age they tend to lose scales near the wing margins.

Host/Larval Food Plants

American Pokeweed — *Phytolacca americana*
Avocado — *Persea americana*
Banana — *Musa* spp.
Black Locust — *Robinia pseudoacacia*
Cabbage — *Brassica oleracea*
Castorbean — *Ricinus communis*
Cherry — *Prunus* spp.
Dandelion — *Taraxacum* spp.
Flamevine — *Pyrostegia venusta*
Golden Polypody — *Phlebodium aureum*
Honeysuckle — *Lonicera* spp.
Magnolia — *Magnolia* spp.
Maple — *Acer* spp.
Mexican Fire Plant — *Euphorbia cyathophora*
Orange — *Citrus* spp.
Paperflower — *Bougainvillea* spp.
Passionflower — *Passiflora* spp.
Plantain — *Plantago* spp.
Southern Needleleaf — *Tillandsia setacea*
Sunflower — *Helianthus* spp.
Toadflax — *Linaria* spp.
Violet — *Viola* spp.
Willow — *Salix* spp.

Purple Passionflower — *Passiflora incarnata*

The Life Cycle

Giant Leopard Moths lay large masses of eggs. The eggs are about 1/32 inch and pearly gray.

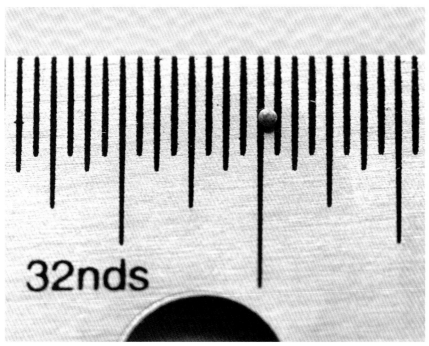

32nds

As the egg develops, it darkens. It takes about 5 to 8 days for the egg to hatch.

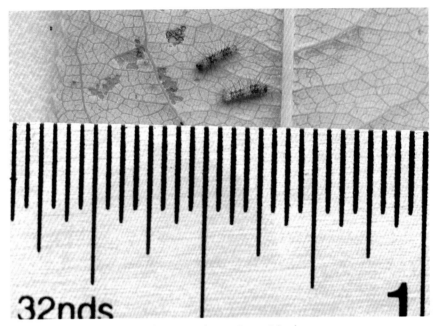

When the caterpillar hatches, it's about 3/32 to 1/8 inch.

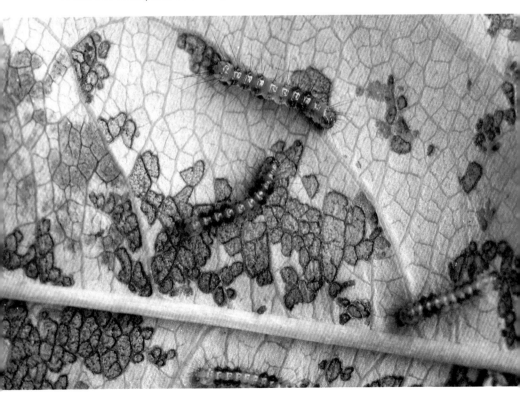

The caterpillars feed at night.

The caterpillars roll up when disturbed. In the last instar, the caterpillar is about 3 inches long. Giant Leopard Moths have one brood in the north and two or more broods in the south. They overwinter as caterpillars.

When the caterpillar makes its cocoon, the cocoon is net-like with thin yellowish silk. Its pupa is black with reddish-brown spiracles.

Adult Food

They nectar on a variety of flowers.

Hickory Tussock Moth

Lophocampa caryae (lah-fah-cam-pah • ka-ree-ah)

Family

Arctiidae (Tiger Moths)
(ark-TEE-ah-day)

Flight period

May–June

Wingspan

1 7/16–2 1/8 inches

Identification

Dorsal/Upperside

The dorsal/upperside forewing is yellow with brown shading and white spots. The hindwing is very pale yellow.

Female

Male

The female has a fatter abdomen and thinner antennae than the male.

Host/Larval Food Plants

American Hornbeam — *Carpinus caroliniana*

Ash — *Fraxinus* spp.

Aspen — *Populus* spp.

Basswood — *Tilia* spp.

Birch — *Betula* spp.

Black Locust — *Robinia pseudoacacia*

Blueberry — *Vaccinium* spp.

Elm — *Ulmus* spp.

Hickory — *Carya* spp.

Hops — *Humulus* spp.

Maple — *Acer* spp.

Oak — *Quercus* spp.

Pecan — *Carya illinoinensis*

Quaking Aspen — *Populus tremuloides*

Raspberry — *Rubus idaeus*

Rose — *Rosa* spp.

Sumac — *Rhus* spp.

Virginia Creeper — *Parthenocissus quinquefolia*

Walnut — *Juglans* spp.

Black Walnut — *Juglans nigra*

The Life Cycle

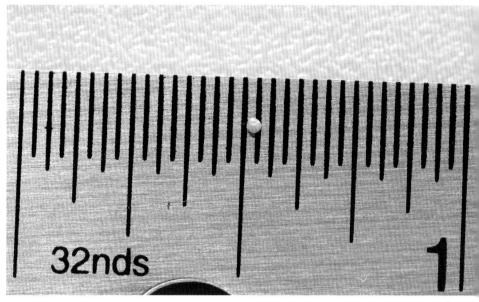

Eggs are laid on the underside of leaves in masses of 50 to several hundred and are each about 1/32 inch and light green.

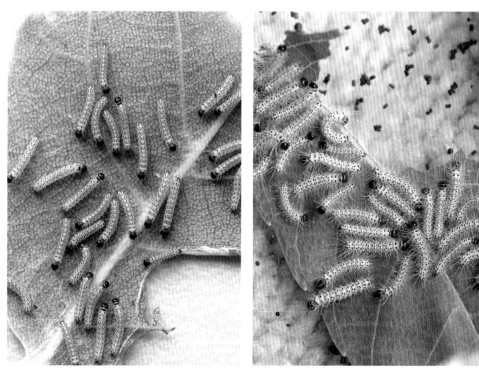

Caterpillars in their early instars stay together.

Use caution when handling caterpillars you are unfamiliar with. Many people may have an allergic reaction when touching a caterpillar, and it may feel like a burning, itchy rash. Cleaning the area with soap and water, dabbing on ammonia or calamine lotion, and then putting ice on it should handle the problem. Some sensitive people could have swelling and feel nauseous and may have to see a doctor.

In the last instar, the caterpillar is about 1¾ inches long. Right before it gets ready to pupate, its back turns brownish.

The cocoons are about 1 inch wide. The moths pupate in cocoons in leaf litter on the ground or under bark and emerge in the spring.

Adult Food

Adults do not have working mouthparts and do not eat.

Spongy Moth ⊘
(formerly known as Gypsy Moth)

Lymantria dispar (ly-mahn-tri-ah • dis-par)

Do not raise Spongy Moths. The reason they've been included is to prevent anyone accidentally raising this species.

Spongy Moths are invasive pests that are a major threat to North American forests. In peak years, the caterpillars can defoliate large sections of forest.

They have been recorded in the U.S. from Maine to as far west as parts of California, and from Minnesota to as far south as Florida. In Canada, they have been recorded in Nova Scotia, New Brunswick, Quebec, Ontario and British Columbia.

Family

Lymantriidae (Tussock Moths) (ly-MAHN-tri-ah-dee)

Flight period

July–August

Wingspan

Male
1 3/16–1 9/16 inches

Female
2 3/16–2 5/8 inches

Identification

Dorsal/Upperside

The dorsal/upperside of the male's forewing is brown with a yellowish overlay and darker brown scalloped lines and spots. The hindwing is yellowish to reddish-brown. The male has a thin abdomen.

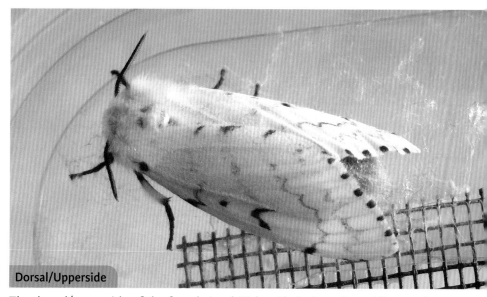

Dorsal/Upperside

The dorsal/upperside of the female is whitish with dark scalloped lines and spots. The female has a large abdomen.

Host/Larval Food Plants

There are over 500 food plants recorded so far. Spongy Moth larvae prefer Oak, but they also feed on Alder, Apple, Basswood, Beech, Birch, Box Elder, Hawthorn, Hazelnut, Hickory, Larch, Mountain Ash, Poplar, Rose Bush, Sumac, Willow and Witch Hazel.

 Spongy Moth larvae are very destructive. In peak years, they can defoliate large sections of forest. They are also a threat to North America's conifer forests. They were deliberately brought to Boston, Massachusetts, from Europe in 1869 for silk production. Unfortunately, some escaped.

The Life Cycle

Spongy Moths have 1 brood each year. The eggs overwinter, and the following year they hatch. The caterpillars are fully grown by May and June. In the last instar, they are about 2 ⅛ inches long.

The caterpillar's hairs are allergenic, especially if they come into contact with eyes or sensitive skin.

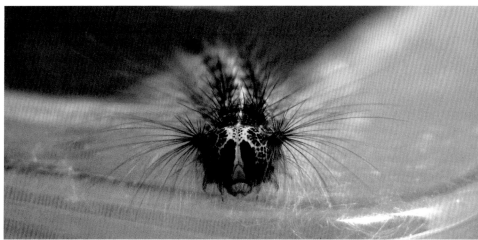

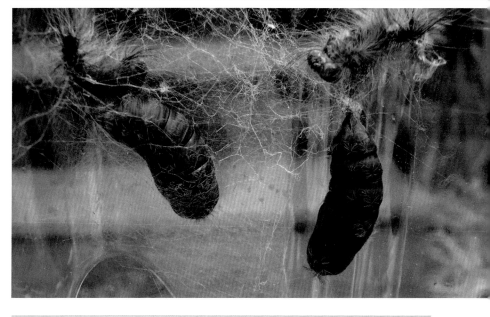

Glossary

Abdomen: The third main body part of a butterfly or moth.

Antenna: Sensory appendage on a butterfly's or moth's head used for touching and smelling. (Plural: antennae)

Aestivate: A type of summer hibernation.

Brood: A generation of young.

Caterpillar: The second stage of a butterfly's and moth's life cycle; this is also called a larva (plural: larvae).

Cell: An area on the wing that is encircled by veins.

Chrysalis: A hard case that lacks a protective covering in which a caterpillar transforms into a butterfly. (Plural: chrysalises) This is also called pupa. (Plural: pupae)

Claspers: Appendages at the end of the male's abdomen that clasp the female during mating.

Cocoon: A silken covering that protects the pupa as it transforms from a caterpillar to a moth.

Cremaster: A structure at the end of the caterpillar's abdomen that contains small hooks and is used to attach the pupa to a silk pad.

Diapause: A state of dormancy, usually in winter, often induced by reduced daylight hours that protects butterflies and moths from long periods of inclement weather.

Diurnal: Active during the day.

Dorsal: The upperside of the butterfly or moth.

Eclose: To emerge from an egg or pupa.

Epidermis: The outermost layer of cells covering the leaves.

Exoskeleton: The hard external covering of the caterpillar, pupa and adult.

Forewings: The pair of wings that are attached to the thorax, closest to the head.

Frass: Caterpillar excrement.

Genus: A group of species that have a significant number of similar or identical characteristics. (Plural: genera)

Hibernaculum: A silken shelter in which caterpillars hibernate or aestivate.

Hindwings: The pair of wings that are attached to the thorax, closest to the abdomen.

Host plants: Specific plants required by the caterpillar for food.

Imago: The adult butterfly or moth.

Instar: Periods of growth between molting.

Larva: The caterpillar stage of butterflies and moths. (Plural: larvae)

Lepidoptera: The order of insects that includes butterflies and moths.

Lepidopterist: A person who studies butterflies and moths.

Life cycle: The stages of changes of an organism from the egg stage to its death as an adult.

Meconium: The first excretion of an adult after eclosing from the pupa.

Metamorphosis: The process of changing from an egg to an adult.

Mesophyll: Most of the tissue between the upper and lower epidermis layers of a leaf.

Molting: The process of shedding the exoskeleton.

Nectar plants: Specific plants required by the adult butterfly or moth for food.

Nocturnal: Active during the night.

Ocelli: The simple eyes of caterpillars, which can only tell whether it is day or night.

Osmeterium: An orangish forked gland behind the head that emits a foul scent to repel predators.

Oviposit: To lay eggs.

Ovum: An egg. (Plural: ova)

Proboscis: A coiled tube that adults use for feeding.

Prolegs: Fleshy legs with very small hooks located on the abdomen.

Puddling: The act of ingesting minerals from damp sand, soil, mulch, etc.

Pupa: A hard case that lacks a protective covering in which a caterpillar transforms into a butterfly or moth. (Plural: pupae)

Pupate: Changing from a caterpillar to a pupa.

Setae: Bristles or hair-like projections on the body.

Spiracles: Holes in the sides of the thorax and abdomen through which a caterpillar receives oxygen.

Spinneret: A silk-producing gland located in the mouthparts of a caterpillar.

Spp.: Multiple species.

Thorax: The second main body part of the butterfly or moth.

Var.: Variety.

Ventral: The underside of the butterfly or moth.

Useful Websites

BugGuide
Website: www.bugguide.net

Bug Life Cycles
Website: www.buglifecycles.com

Butterflies and Moths of North America
Website: www.butterfliesandmoths.org

Butterfly Fun Facts
Website: www.butterfly-fun-facts.com

Monarch Watch
Website: www.monarchwatch.org
Email: monarch@ku.edu
Blog: www.monarchwatch.org/blog
Facebook: www.facebook.com/monarchwatch
Twitter: www.twitter.com/monarchwatch
Shop: shop.monarchwatch.org
Milkweed Market: www.monarchwatch.org/milkweed/market
Free Milkweeds: www.monarchwatch.org/bring-back-the-monarchs
/milkweed/free-milkweeds/
Donate: www.monarchwatch.org/donate

Moth Photographers Group
Website: www.mothphotographersgroup.msstate.edu

North American Butterfly Association
Website: www.naba.org
4 Delaware Road
Morristown, NJ 07960
Email: naba@naba.org

Bibliography

General:

Brock, Jim P., and Kaufman, Kenn. 2003. *Kaufman Focus Guides: Butterflies of North America*. Boston, MA: Houghton Mifflin.

BugGuide
Website: www.bugguide.net

Bug Life Cycles
Website: www.buglifecycles.com

Butterflies and Moths of North America
Website: www.butterfliesandmoths.org

Covell, Charles V. Jr. 2005. *A Field Guide to Moths of Eastern North America*. Martinsville, VA: Virginia Museum of Natural History.

Daniels, Jaret C. 2005. *Butterflies of Michigan: Field Guide*. Cambridge, MN: Adventure Publications, Inc.

Douglas, Matthew M. & Douglas, Jonathan M. 2005. *Butterflies of the Great Lakes Region*. Ann Arbor, MI: The University of Michigan Press.

Nielsen, Mogens C. 1999. *Michigan Butterflies and Skippers*. East Lansing, MI: Michigan State University Extension.

Pasternak, Carol. 2019. *How to Raise Monarch Butterflies: A Step-by-Step Guide for Kids*. Richmond Hill, ON: Firefly Books.

Scott, James A. 1986. *The Butterflies of North America: A Natural History and Field Guide*. Stanford, CA: Stanford University Press.

Tuskes, Paul M., Tuttle, James P., and Collins, Michael M. 1996. *The Wild Silk Moths of North America: A Natural History of the Saturniidae of the United States and Canada*. Ithaca, NY: Cornell University Press.

Tuttle, James P. 2007. *The Hawk Moths of North America: A Natural History Study of the Sphingidae of the United States and Canada*. Lawrence, KS: Allen Press.

Wagner, David L. 2005. *Caterpillars of Eastern North America*. Princeton, NJ: Princeton University Press.

Acknowledgments

I would like to thank my father and mother (John Sattler and Margaret Sattler) for teaching me to respect and love all that God has created. It is this love that has enabled me to devote my life to studying butterflies and moths.

Photo Credits

Photographs are copyright Brenda Sattler, except as noted below:

Angela Gross: 40 (Tiger Swallowtail – bottom), 298 (Cecropia Moth), 299 (Cecropia Moth – top and bottom); Berry Nall: 174 (Julia Heliconian caterpillar – top), 216 (green Queen chrysalis – right); Burris & Richards (www.ButterflyNature.com): 133 (Baltimore Checkerspot eggs – top), 161 (Great Spangled Fritillary eggs – top and bottom); Carol Clements: 162 (Great Spangled Fritillary caterpillar – bottom); D. H. Janzen: 91 (Great Southern White caterpillars – top and bottom); David M. Wright: 119 (Summer Azure egg – top), 120 (Summer Azure pupae – bottom); Dunia Garcia: 92 (Great Southern White caterpillar – top); Glenn M. Richardson: 154 (Eastern Comma eggs – top and bottom), 155 (Eastern Comma caterpillar – top and bottom), 162 (Great Spangled Fritillary caterpillar – top); Jan Dauphin: 65 (Polydamas Swallowtail chrysalis – bottom); Jaret C. Daniels, Ph.D.: 92 (Great Southern White caterpillar – bottom), 265 (Zebra Heliconian caterpillar – bottom); Marcie O'Connor (www.aprairiehaven.com): 197 (Mourning Cloak chrysalis – top); NC Division of Parks and Recreation, photo by Ed Corey: 149 (Common Wood Nymph caterpillar); Peter Bryant: 195 (Mourning Cloak red eggs – middle); Rose Maschek: 209 (Pearl Crescent laying eggs – bottom); William E. Flores: 64 (Polydamas Swallowtail caterpillars – top left and top right)

Front Cover: Brenda Sattler

Back Cover: Brenda Sattler (Monarch photos)

About the Author

Brenda Dziedzic is a co-founder and president of the Southeast Michigan Butterfly Association (SEMBA), the founder of "Brenda's Butterfly Habitat" butterfly house, a Monarch Watch Conservation Specialist for Monarch Watch and a member of the North American Butterfly Association (NABA) and the Wildflower Association of Michigan (WAM). She's an Advanced Master Gardener and was named Wayne County's 2007 Master Gardener of the Year by Michigan State University Extension. The Master Gardener Association of Wayne County (MGAWC) awarded Brenda the 2008 Dean Krauskopf, Ph.D. Educational Outreach Award. She received gold President's Volunteer Service Awards in 2014, 2015, 2016 and 2017 and the President's Lifetime Achievement Award in January 2016. In June 2016, the U.S. House of Representatives awarded her a Certificate of Special Congressional Recognition.

Brenda has lectured widely on the topic of butterfly and moth gardening, and she has made numerous appearances on both television and radio.

Brenda's yard is certified as a Native Butterfly Garden by SEMBA, a Monarch Waystation by Monarch Watch and a Wildlife Habitat by the National Wildlife Federation.

Brenda can be contacted at brendad1@ameritech.net.

This book can be purchased at your local bookstore, online or in bulk from Firefly Books (contact service@fireflybooks.com). Firefly Books will give bulk discounts to conservation groups.

Host/Larval Food Plant Index

Nannyberry 20
Nasturtium 82, 90
Nasturtium officinale 90, 92
Nettle 152, 220, 230
Nettletree 308
New England Aster 209
New Jersey Tea 118

Oak 238, 308, 322, 328, 378, 384
Ocotillo 294
Orange 370
Oxypolis filiformis 26

Palm 308
Paper Birch 194
Paperflower 370
Parietaria pensylvanica 230
Parsley 26
Parthenocissus quinquefolia 378
Passiflora spp. 166, 167, 264, 370
    incarnata 370
Passionflower 370
Passion-Vine 166, 167, 172, 264
Pastinaca sativa 26
Pawpaw 76
Pear 238, 300, 308
Pearly Everlasting 124
Pecan 378
Pedicularis canadensis 132
Pennsylvania Pellitory 230
Penstemon hirsutus 132

Pentas spp. 362
    lanceolata 362
Peppergrass 82, 90
Persea spp.
    americana 370
    borbonia 68, 308
Persimmon 314
Petroselinum crispum spp. 26
Phlebodium aureum 370
Phyla spp. 138
Phytolacca americana 370
Pipevine 62
Pipturus albidus 230
Piscidia piscipula 308
Plantago spp. 138, 200, 370
    lanceolata 132, 139
Plantain 138, 200, 370
Plum 300
Poa spp. 148
Polanisia dodecandra 90
Poplar 194, 238, 256, 308, 384
Populus spp. 36, 194, 238, 256, 308, 378
Populus tremuloides 378
Privet 294
Prosopis spp. 308
Prunus spp. 36, 118, 238, 294, 300, 308, 336, 370
    serotina 238
    virginiana 19
Pseudognaphalium obtusifolium 124
Ptelea trifoliata 36, 44

Ptilimnium capillaceum 26
Purple Passionflower 370
Purpletop Tridens 148
Pussytoes 124
Pussy Willow 239
Pyrostegia venusta 370
Pyrus spp. 238, 300, 308

Quaking Aspen 378
Queen Anne's Lace 26
Quercus spp. 238, 308, 322, 328, 378
    laevis 342
    muehlenbergii 322, 328

Radish 82
Raphanus sativus 82
Raspberry 308, 378
Redbay 68, 308
Redbud 308
Red Clover 96, 104, 144
Red Mangrove 308
Red Maple 342
Redwhisker Clammyweed 90
Rhizophora mangle 308
Rhododendron spp. 308
Rhus spp. 118, 314, 378
    typhina 20
Ribes spp. 308
Ricinus communis 370
Robinia pseudoacacia 278, 370, 378
Rosa spp. 308, 378
Rose 308, 378
Rose Bush 384
Royal Poinciana 308

Butterfly and Moth Index